DORSETT'S TREATISE

ON

AGRICULTURE,

IN ALL ITS VARIOUS BRANCHES,

FROM

THIRTY YEARS' PRACTICAL EXPERIENCE.

BY FOLSOM DORSETT.

CHICAGO:
ROUNDS & JAMES, STEAM BOOK AND JOB PRINTERS.
1867.

TO THE

FARMERS' TOWNSHIP CLUB ORGANIZATION,

FOR THE

Advancement of a more Perfect Knowledge of Agriculture,

THIS BOOK IS RESPECTFULLY DEDICATED,

BY YOUR FRIEND,

FOLSOM DORSETT.

ERRATA.

Hog Culture,	Page 63
Distribution of Time,	" 226
Supplement—"Making Pure Butter,"	" 217
For "affection," read "affliction,"	" 57
For "affect," read "effect,"	" 66
For "that should breeding in and in be tolerated," read "that breeding in and in should not be tolerated,"	" 90
For "the best elements," read "the best laws,"	" 93
For "from," read "four,"	" 99
The lanes are not fenced in round the Model Farm,	" 157

INDEX.

PREFACE.

The design of this work is to furnish a comprehensive treatise on Agriculture, as deduced from an experience of thirty years cultivating the soil, ten years in Maine, and twenty in Central Illinois, and a residence of ten years in Chicago, where I have been familiar with the quality and condition of the produce of the West, as it has come forward to Chicago for a market. And while I am pleased to say there was much sold for good prices, being of good quality, I regret to say there was more of the medium and poorer qualities, sold, to pay the producer but little or no profit. It is true the elements might have injured some of this produce to lessen the prices.

Under these existing features, as to grades, qualities and condition, the produce coming to market, from the same locality of soils and climate, my mind was drawn to take issue on the subject of the good, medium, and pure culture of the soil, producing the results I have witnessed on the sale of these products, both animal and vegetable, grown in the West.

After much reflection upon this important subject, and having an inborn desire to see the farmers have more uniformity in their prosperity from their labors, I resolved to write out my views and sentiments, from the stand point of my practical labors on agriculture, and the knowledge by theory, of the physical and chemical laws of animals and plants, with their relations so inseparably existing; and so perfectly harmonious are their transmutations performed by the inscrutable wisdom of an all wise Creator, were these rich bountiful provisions made for the support of His people. And the more faithfully will the farmers bend their minds to learn these great living truths, the more certain will prosperity attend their labors to secure larger rewards for their better husbandry. Under the guiding rule that animals and plants must equally have food from nature's great store house, man being endowed with the highest type of wisdom on earth, is specially required to see that neither shall suffer for great want, while under his immediate care and protection. And all other pursuits of life will be stimulated to higher action, in all their needful labors, so essential to happiness.

In conclusion, I would most respectfully add, that if the principal features laid down in this work, are sought after, and adopted by the farmers, as a rule of action, in the culture of their animals and plants, I feel sanguine to say the results will prove to be less in amount of labor, more in wealth, and a larger degree of health, which are the essential stimulants to elevate humanity to a higher source of happiness. And finally, may the author indulge the hope, that this book may receive a fair and impartial perusal by the farmers of the West, omitting all the imperfections therein contained. Believing it is from the hand that hath striven hard upward through the rugged paths of life, devoted to agriculture, as it was thirty years ago, on the prairies of Illinois, where in many places the Indian trails showed evidence of recent occupation.

With these desultory remarks, I cheerfully submit it in a special manner, to the cultivators of the soil.

Your Friend,

FOLSOM DORSETT.

THE FARMER'S GUIDE.

CHAPTER I.

HOME AND ITS SURROUNDINGS.

NO word, in the language of civilization, has so many *endearing* ties as that of *home*. Within its boundaries are rest from toil and oppressive cares of life, tender sympathy and sheltering love, and implicit confidence as found no where else on earth.

There is a charm in the word *home* which calls up memories from the long buried past, that fill the mind with all that is pure and enduring in our lives, and we live over again, in imagination, the happy scenes of childhood, so full of joy, so free from care.

What sweet and hallowed associations cluster round the home circle. There we find the father's care, the mother's love, and the brothers' and sisters' affection. The storms of life may beat upon us, while out in the world battling with its cares, and perplexities; but, if we have a home, it is to us a city of refuge; where our wearied limbs and aching hearts can find rest and tranquility. Well we may exclaim, what dear and sacred places they are! and how kind in our Heavenly Father to implant in our breast such a love for them.

But my friends who cultivate the soil; in order to make your homes replete with the comforts of wealth, beauty and *health*, special pains should be taken in laying out five acres of ground, more or less, surrounding your house, so arranged to give you a vegetable garden affording all the rich vegetables so healthful and necessary for your family—then the balance of this ground suitably and tastefully divided for your small fruits in berries, with plums, peaches, pears, crab apples, and your substantial fruit, the orchard of apples, and last though not least, there should be laid off first, ground fronting your house as a lawn interspersed with your flowers, evergreens, and such ornamental trees as your family may desire; of course you will have the tasty walks necessary for beauty and comfort. This should all be enclosed with a neat substantial fence, with the front beautified to correspond with the rich view your house must have, when you have your surroundings growing onward to a higher state of perfection.

Hence it is, we shall see with these rich flowers and ornamental trees, with these high scented perfumes being wafted by every breeze, so well designed to energize and stimulate the farmers to cultivate their lands and do all their husbandry in the best possible manner, showing the utility in cultivating the fields well, then all will join hands with beautifying and advancing their home grounds.

The next object under consideration, for the farmer to have, is a good ventilated cellar, if not under his whole house, under a part of it at least, so at all times of the year, he can have a place for vegetables; if your ground is level, raise your house three feet, put an embankment round it, windows in the cellar, giving free ventilation of pure air, so all necessary to health. No house in our country should be permitted to rest on the ground, thereby endangering the life of its inhabitants. Friends, this is no idle talk, to gratify curiosity; it is a reality, and worthy of your highest consideration, especially in the summer season, when vegetable and animal matter is under a hasty decomposition, to say the least about it, when stagnant, it must create disease. Hence the importance of ventilation where people are sleeping. A word to the wise is sufficient on this subject.

Economy, in saving the floor joist from rotting, should induce all to raise their houses from the ground, say nothing of more urgent requirements.

As there are many forms and fashions in building houses, and many inconvenient for the room taken up, I hope it may not seem out of place for me to give my views on a farmer's house.

As I have said before, utility and beauty should at all times go together; or, in other words, taste and labor saving conveniences should be strictly adhered to, and the best plans after much reflection should be adopted. It would be well to consult the wife's feelings in regard to some of the rooms and pantrys, for after the house is completed, it cannot be so well attended to. You will please to notice my plans for two houses, which I have attached to my model farm, which I desire all who are intending to build houses, to make an examination as to size, form and division of rooms, to give comfort and ease, so desirable to all having to do in the farmer's house.

The small house is constructed for a small family, with small means, and situated so that a front can be put up any time, forming by the addition a neat sizeable house as though all were put up at one time. When you are building, it is just as cheap to build with an eye single to symmetry of form and taste, as otherwise, and whenever you may wish to sell, you can always get well paid for your good judgment; so with all you may do on your farm. All I have to say further in regard to the improvements, is a good sized dining-room, with kitchen, well, and cistern of rain water, and bath room should be constructed as I have represented, and the bath house, let me say to all farmers, that no family living deserve and require bathing so often as him who has to do with cultivating the soil, and the sooner you add this to your homestead, the sooner and more certain by this bathing will you be cleansed, and your flesh will breathe free, to put all the functions of the body in a healthy condition, so essential to insure good health.

Now the out-houses, beginning with wood-house. No one will deny the utility of this, when in a cold, sleeting, drifting snow storm, or without the snow, will for one day want to live without it. A part of this wood-house divided, will serve for your work shop for doing any repairs that often happen to farm utensils, every farmer wants his work room, with plenty of good seasoned wood on hand to make these repairs, without going miles to get these trifling jobs done — and here is the place for all your tools, when not in special use. I need not dwell on this point, for it is apparent to all, that all tools should be under cover. The privy is a small habitation, full of many comforts which my pen is not able to express; only have the passage-ways made pleasant, so that life is not endangered by the voyage to it.

The smoke-house requires care in its construction, the bars to hang the meat upon should not be placed too low, ten feet will answer. The oven should be made with brick, laid open, so as to let the smoke through freely and keep back the heat. Brick or stone are the best for this purpose. For the house you also want brick or stone,— or if wood, line the walls with blue clay; this will be warm in winter and cool in summer. Two small windows are necessary for ventilation; by having the house dark, you can keep your meat through the warm weather, by having smoke put in twice a week, leaving the windows open a little when you have the smoke in.

On reflection I think the farmers who have not these buildings erected, to set them in a line and connect them, when making the smoke house, tool and work shop, and house with kettle to cook food for the hogs, having all these buildings adjoining, and serve as a fence on the line of the rest of your back yard, from your house towards your barn ; this with your hog pens next to your barn-yard, would serve well to break off the wind while passing to your barn, so available in winter time. These improvements you can make, as time and means will permit.

CHAPTER II.

BARN AND SHEDS FOR STOCK.

These buildings should be made, in size and extent, to correspond with the size of your farm, and the stock you intend keeping. Base your farm one hundred and sixty acres—I would build the barn fifty by thirty-six feet—stable on one side for horses, ground mow for hay on the other side, and over the floor and horses I would have for hay, and all the rye and oats in bundles, for cutting up for food for your horses and calves.

Then on the outside of the barn, by the ground mow side, you should have a shed to hold your special stock of steers you are fattening, with you bull, cows and calves, having a partition from your other stock; your yard should be large enough to feed one hundred head of cattle, with a tight fence high enough to make the back of a shed, you should have around your yard, excepting gate-ways; these sheds should be roofed over, and boarded in front, so as to let stock pass under, but for cold sleeting storms, sections should be made, to close up this front, at any time by sliding these sections long to form an entire front; by this means you can separate your stock whenever you desire to —so essential with your cows when coming in, and all other needful changes you so often may want to make.

Oh! how much suffering I have seen by farmers not having the facilities to give aid and comfort to cows, calves and other stock in time of need. If there are any malicious animals in your yard that are dangerous to injure other cattle, put them in prison so they can do no damage; these measures should be adopted and carried out, taking out these cross malignant cattle, and the balance you can put into pens free from doing any harm; these duties you owe to yourself as a matter of economy, and a higher duty you have to protect your domestic animals that are under your care, to see they are kept from the tortures and wounds that give so much pain where much loss and even death is the result, by these too often neglects, occasioned by the ommission of the farmers. All that is wanted, is a due weight of wise reflection to make your homes and surroundings valuable in wealth, full of rich comforts of health and blessings, that would meet the admiration of all other social business of life, and especially those residing in cities where those rich treasures cannot so cheaply be afforded.

CHAPTER III.

VEGETABLE AND FRUIT GARDENS.

The amount of rich vegetables and fruits that can be cultivated and grown upon five acres of land, surrounding the farmer's home, has seldom if ever been fully comprehended as to quality and quantity. The cause of this great and lamentable neglect, I will in kindness assign to others, what I am reluctantly obliged to take myself, while cultivating the soil. Thus it was then, and it is so with the farmers now, evidently for the want of an energetic, reflecting mind, to arouse them up to a true sense of their best interests, affording such rich comforts in health and prosperity, to their families. And now let me cheerfully ask, who will be the first in the farming districts of the west, to take measures to carry out the plans I have recommended in this essay—so essential to the farmers, and conferring rich blessings to all branches of industry, by furnishing fresh vegetables and fruits, thereby laying just claims upon them, for a renewed vigorous taxation of their mind and muscle, that will produce a larger amount of manufactured wares so as to equalize the benefits arising from the better cultivation of the soil of our country. Advance these two great life-sustaining interests, and civilization will have taken a long march forward to a higher sphere of action.

Well may the farmers feel proud and elevated, when they are cultivating their gardens of vegetables, fruits and flowers, that so beautifully surround their dwellings, for they are performing the same Heaven-born, laudable duties, that our first parents were commissioned to perform in that hallowed spot, the Garden of Eden, by the great all wise Creator, who was pleased to dedicate it with that ever memorable name, Paradise—fresh from their Creator-Father. We can faintly imagine the glow of splendor and radiant beauty, that must have pervaded that ever memorable time when nature was fresh in her newness of existence.

What hallowed ground. But my friends, with all these rich blessings so freely bestowed upon our first parents, I would kindly ask the question, if the cultivators of the soil of our country, in a temporal sense at least, have not blessings equally as great, and should we not feel thankful to the same all wise and beneficent Parent, for casting our lives in such a land, full of all the natural resources that mind and muscle can desire. Let them diligently work together, and the prosperity of our country none are able to appreciate its future greatness, for which we should ever feel grateful, and take every pains to make our gardens smile and fairly groan with burdens of rich vegetables and fruits, thereby fulfilling the just requirements of all who cultivate the soil as a profession.

On this train of thought my mind is called to the

fact, that the farmers can have with very little extra expense, vegetables from one month to six weeks earlier by making a hot bed in the fall, by digging out a trench, say twenty to forty feet long, five feet wide by twenty inches deep,—then take fresh manures, fill it nearly full, and cover this over with six inches of the mixture of this soil; if a sandy clay loam, the better. Put up a bulk head at the north side and ends of this bed, with boards four feet high to shelter it from the winds. Before hard freezing, cover it over with straw two feet deep. At the January thaw, take off the straw and let it have some rain or melted snow on it; then return the straw again, and let it remain on the bed until the first of March, when you can remove it altogether. Take a bushel of lime, mix it with a bushel of old manure, and pulverize this with the top soil on your hot bed. It would be well to incline it to the south a little.

The seeds most desirable to plant are the Early Kidney Potatoes, early Peas and Beans, choice Tomatoes, Sweet Corn, Crook Neck Squash, and Sweet Potato. These all can be successfully propagated by planting them in rows, three inches apart. Plant the Potatoes six inches apart. This bed should be protected by glass costing ten cents per foot, and to those who can afford it, it will pay the best interest on the same amount invested. As soon as the weather will permit in the spring, have your beds made in your garden, where you should, the fall before, have put on six inches deep of horse, cattle, and hog manure, and then pulverize and subsoil down sixteen inches, turning this manure under, having the soil well mixed and thoroughly pulverized. Then take your plants from the hot bed, and set them carefully out. With proper tending, you will have the pleasure of having some of those vegetables by the middle of May. When you transplant, take a knife to cut the dirt. The expense of this hot bed arrangement will take one day's labor to dig the trench, put the manure in, and cover it over, and two days to take up plants and set them out.

If you have a twenty feet bed, the glass will cost ten dollars, and will last you a life-time, and every year you can have your hot bed, with the luxuries of early vegetables, at a cost the first year of only twenty dollars, and after that a yearly expense of five dollars. What family would refuse this amount for the rich vegetables, so early in the season, when they are so much needed. And what farmer in the west, who is blest with a family, will neglect to prepare his garden in the fall, by subsoiling it down sixteen inches, after having spread on six inches of manure. Reflect for a moment that the manure is to be well stirred up with sixteen inches of soil, so you need have no fears of its being too rich. One acre of land cultivated as I have recommended, will produce three hundred dollars in vegetables, and your family will be more healthy throughout the year. May the farmers look at it in a right light, and go forward to obtain the results that will follow the labors I have suggested on garden culture

CHAPTER IV.

TOWNSHIP ORGANIZATIONS.

Township organization for agriculture should be adopted, for the advancement of a more perfect knowledge in cultivating the soil of our country.

It is true the County and State Agricultural Societies have done much in many respects to advance the interests of agriculture.

But with all their assiduous labors so faithfully bestowed, it must seem on mature reflection, that the true object in view, and sought after, can never be obtained, as constituted by the County and State Societies at this present time, from the fact, the farmers contesting for the best quality and quantities of grains, do generally live at a distance from each other.

Hence, the impossibility of their having an equal chance in regard to the elements, that must and do favor one more than the other at certain times, for these cogent reasons, a fair estimation of the true culture of the soil cannot be successfully arrived at.

Hence, I am, by much reflection persuaded that the only way a true test can ever be ascertained, what soils are able to bear, and by actual demonstrations thoroughly made by farmers, living side by side, having the same soil, climate, showers, droughts and all incidental ills and favors that may arise during the season, standing now to all appearances upon a fair footing. Must come the sure test with these two farmers, and so on with others in the same situation through the country, to make their trial tests in cultivating their wheat, corn, &c., in ways by stipulation, or by their own volition, keeping a true record of all manures, labor, depth of plowing, kind and condition of the soil, kind of seed, when sown and what manner of cultivation &c., and how secured from the weather.

Fellow farmers of our country and especially in the west, where I have cultivated the soil a long time, don't this seem to be the most available way and means to find out the highest resources of the soil, with the smallest amount of labor and money expended which is the highest aim of all industry under the tuition of our countries best instruction.

Hence, farmers adopt the organization system, by choosing a Chairman and Secretary—selecting a good board of referees for adjusting all matters of interest that may arise, conferring a spirit of assimilation to bring out, by your laudable exertions in cultivating your farms under the most favorable circumstances, for the promotion of their united interest of cultivating the soil, on a practical scientific basis, under the auspices of your new organization by townships.

Who will respond and compete at the County and

State Fairs, taking the best samples as awarded by your own board of referees, in your grains, fruits and animals, manifesting a liberal spirit to imitate those that have succeeded in the towns by their best culture of what was assigned them for competition, having all strictly done, to advance the great cause of your noble profession.

In conclusian, let me advise you to procure the best works on agriculture, emanating from a practical experience and scientific investigation on the physical and chemical laws of animals and plants, that you may learn to supply the proper food, that in their nature they will require and demand for their full constitutional growth.

Farmers of the west, I submit these remarks for your most candid and worthy consideration, hoping from your mature reflection, you will find favor in the plans of township organization for the special purpose that it will insure you greater rewards from your meritorious labors in tilling the soil of our country, from whence all its primary prosperity must flow.

CHAPTER V.

INDIAN CORN

Is the greatest material product cultivated in our country, and has double the rich supporting qualities for fattening all animals, and especially hogs, than any other grain in proportion to the cost of cultivation.

Well did the justly celebrated horticulturalist *Linœus*, give it the true botanical name from the Greek word zoa, which signifies *to live;* and this reminds me of the advice that an old settler gave me, when I first came to the State of Illinois, who said to me, raise plenty of corn, for all can live on it, which I have found to be measurably true; and well has our all wise beneficent *Creator*, made a wide range of latitude for the possible cultivation of the rich oily product, for we find it growing in the low vallies of the Amazon, South America and on the plains of Mexico, and, so on up to the higher latitude of the Canadas.

But no where in this wide range of country, can we find as much land having the available climate and natural richness of soils for sustaining and maturing so large in quantity, and sound in quality, as in the Western States, where we find by the agricultural report at Washington, that over four hundred millions of bushels of corn was produced in nine western states, by common cultivation in 1864, begining with Illinois, 138,356,135; Ohio, 68,202,641; Indiana, 74,284,363; Iowa, 55,261,240; Missouri, 36,635,011; Michigan, 11,088,801; Wisconsin, 10,087,053; Young Minnesota, 4,674,329, and Young Kansas, 4,673,081. This was sold at an average of one dollar per bushel.

Deep plowing, say twelve inches, can be done with high post plows, on our prairie soil. By taking a lighter land you can plow one and a half acres per day; if not this way, sub soil your ground, making light work for two teams; let your tall horse or mule, or even oxen, go in the furrow to balance your double trees.

Now friends, you have your soil twelve inches deep, with all the offal plowed well under, and you are all ready to plant your corn, this being the crop we are now treating upon. But there has come a heavy rain, and the water stands all over in a muck, so you cannot plant for several days. But look here, have we not plowed our ground twelve inches deep? True. We will go out and see, and sure enough this deep plowing has let the surplus water down, and we can plant to-morrow, and so we do, and it works splendidly. This certainly is an advantage for planting. But is this all for our deep plowing; no indeed, there is better yet. And to those who may not realize the fact, I will tell them that in the months of July and August and even until it has made its growth, to my knowledge, for the past thirty years, the corn suffers very much, and at times and places it is almost a failure, as we can see by the low average reported, all for the want of deep plowing — and this twelve inches with proper tending, will save your corn, from the fact that this loose soil below the roots where the moisture lies at the bottom of this plowing, and the roots by the laws of nature will draw this moisture made rich by the vegetable matter you plowed under last fall, small stubble—or in the spring as it is unfortunately done by many farmers.

Some may say we don't get any benefit from what we have plowed under, it is so deep. Let me say that these dry months will surely bring it all up, for the sun attracts it very much by the roots of the plant. There is a mistaken idea about the roots of plants. They will grow down much deeper if the soil is plowed to let them grow, and I know that it is essential to all plants, and most with the luxuriant corn, that has to make a full crop fifteen thousand pounds of vegetable substance, consisting of starch, sugar, oil and woody fibre, and all from the production of fifty to one hundred bushels of the rich golden corn.

In this same report from Washington, we also find in the twenty-one loyal states, there was a production of five hundred and thirty million bushels of corn from seventeen millions of acres, making an average of thirty bushels per acre, and I am sorry to find that our nine western states, only made a fraction over twenty-nine bushels per acre, and in 1863 on account of the drought, only an average of twenty-three bushels per acre in the west.

How shall this be increased on an average to fifty bushels per acre in the western states? From my experience and study into the natural inorganic elements of the soil, and the constituent organic food plants must have furnished to the soil, where plants are cultivated, in order to ensure a full harvest.

Under these considerations I would imperatively recommend to the farmers of the west to adopt the following rules and strictly adhere to them:

First—Make a division of your land in proportion to the quantities of the kind you want to cultivate, specially reserving one piece to seed with clover, as a legal tender to regulate and supply the balances that your other plants require from time to time; your better judgment should dictate which crop you will plant first, but always bear in mind if you cultivate wheat, it should follow clover, supplying the rich food in time so essential to insure a full harvest. Then you should plow your ground twelve inches deep, turning under all vegetable matter left on the field after harvest, and all the manures arising from your stock—always put your manure on your corn and meadow lands, and by this course of culture, your wheat, oats and rye will find strength to hold their own.

Now some farmers, may think this deep plowing would be unnecessary—to all such, I would briefly say why it is essential, and hope I shall be able to convince them that it is the only sure way they have to gather a good sound harvest, having the quantity that true culture will merit.

It would be well for the farmers of our country, and especially of the west, to take a fair comprehensive view of the corn culture; the relation it bears to the wealth of our country under all its multiplied forms of consumption, of which I will here mention some of the most prominent, viz:

The superior qualities it has for fattening our animals (for food,) and especially the hundreds of millions of bushels consumed yearly on the hog and beef product, so rich in substance that no other vegetable product can ever be raised to take its place.

Then the important attachments it has by a large number of the human family, for its rich farina puddings, more delicate in looks and taste than any farinaceous flours, and who will not eat the pure corn cake, or the meal when well mixed with rye, making such delicious bread and so excellent, containing all the anti-dyspeptic qualities, which should warrant a large consumption throughout our entire country.

Then again there are large quantities manufactured into starch, that no other material can be found so available to make the article so cheaply for its goodness.

Then too, we see quite a large quantity taken and manufactured for chemical purposes, which are essential and necessary, and a blessing to mankind.

And now last, and I am sorry not least, a very large amount of this rich life sustaining food, as bread for man, and all other consistent beneficial purposes is taken and manufactured into whisky, which by its cheapness, being made near where the corn is produced will increase the consumption in many localities, so that misery and vice will more or less abound from the bitter effects of cheap whisky; and I have only to say, I wish the people of our country would look at this matter in its true light, and those engaged in this branch of industrial labor, would rise up as one man, and firmly, and irrevocably say, that henceforth we will not make any more whisky to be used to destroy the mind and happiness of our own kindred and fellow beings.

The exhaustive powers of the corn product on the soil is extensive, and every farmer should know the effect it has upon the soil, that they may be able to supply the organic elements as food to insure a full product.

In the commencement of this work, I have made a few succinct remarks in relation to the constituent organic elements, necessary to be in soils, so with proper cultivation the farmers have a grounded right to expect a good crop.

Now friends, I know you want to raise at least fifty bushels of corn per acre, and from my own experience, you ought to cultivate your rich land to raise eighty to one hundred bushels per acre, but set it at fifty—and when your corn is full in the milk, you have about ten thousand pounds of substance per acre on your grounds, consisting nearly half each of carbon and oxygen—with the balance of hydrogen and nitrogen—being the organic elements of the plants, with a small trace of inorganic as mineral, equal to the amount if the whole were burned up, and nothing but the ashes were left.

You will notice, that this ten thousand pounds of corn substance, has been cultivated and raised out of the ground, with its splendid green foliage, with its rich fruits, hanging so firm and stately, will soon turn to its golden harvest, to reward the farmers of our country.

Reflect for a moment, that this is the proceeds from eight pounds of seed, and well may the farmers have an earnest desire, to know how the soil can be cultivated to insure this large amount of product for the least labor expended.

And my practical experience, reflections and studies on the physical laws of animals and plants —tells me in sentiments that cannot be controverted, that the soil after the two first crops, must have all the vegetable offal, with all the manures from every source, returned back to the soil, cultivated and plowed under twelve inches, well harrowed and pulverized, that the soil may have the power and ability to receive and distribute all the rains, dews, air, heat and light, elements of strength and food from nature's bountiful store-house, all to stay, protect and nourish her seed intended for the farmer.

BENEFITS OF DEEP PLOWING.

From the most scientific investigations made, we have the evident fact, that the soil should be plowed twelve inches deep, and thoroughly pulverized especially for raising corn, that requires strong rich mellow soil, made so by all available means of turning under all the vegetable substances and never suffer any to be burned up under any circumstances—with all the manures that can be furnished to give life and vigor to the constitutional elements of the soil.

The importance of deep plowing is manifested in the spring, when heavy rains are frequent, after you have planted, with this deep culture, the surplus water will sink below your seed, and rest if not run off on the base of your plowing, until the plants will need it when the top soil becomes dry.

With this twelve inches of mellow soil, ready to receive the seed by its friable porous condition, all the rains, dews, light and heat, must send the corn plant forward through July and August with strength and substance that must insure a large harvest, that will exceed the fifty bushels per acre, and with fair prospects of eighty. But in order to realize these rich results, the farmer must adhere to these suggestions, and carry them all forward, take the utmost care in securing your seed corn, and this year will require extra pains, for much of the corn raised this year will not answer for seed, having lost its germinating qualities; I would recommend the farmers to take a sample of the seed they intend to plant, and put some soil into a box and have it stand in a suitable place, warm enough to have the seed sprout, and if it don't come readily, you can experiment until you find the right kind, this will save you great loss and trouble by having to replant.

You will see in my remarks on procuring good seeds, the stress I put on seed corn. I will only repeat here the fact, that more importance is attached to the propagating and saving pure sound seeds, in a proper healthy manner, ready when seed time comes, that you have an undoubted assurance that your seeds are full of germinating life, is an unfailing special duty that rests upon the farmers, and I have full confidence, that all who will read this Essay, will comply with the instructions I have given on securing pure ripe seeds.

The preferable way of planting is by machines, especially if the soil is pulverized, for it lays the seed together at one depth, pressing the soil gently so the seed will feel the soil at once, and if in a dry time, the machine is far the best, also preventing the birds and squirrels from taking up the seed, and it leaves the ground well to cultivate, being little depressed, so that the harrow can throw a little mellow earth around the corn, to cover up the young weeds. I would put a light, fine long-tooth harrow in a double V, so as to expand or contract as you may desire.

In this mellow soil, I would use the fine double Cultivator, taking one row at a time for the first after the harrow, and perhaps the second will do as well, and if you have no other, the third time you can use the same molds in a single frame, with means to extend the breadth, or contract, as required.

I would leave my last culture around the corn dishing, that when the showers come in the Summer, through the months of July and August, when the plants need their strongest nourishing food, and the water from these showers, caught up by these small basins which you have made around the plants, enabling the roots, by the deep pulverized condition of the soil, to drink freely of that rich lactescent organic fluid, that comes to sustain and give life and vigor to the famishing plants, and by means of the farmer's better cultivation in preparing his soil, with all the abilities that scientific investigations are being furnished to the cultivators of the soil, setting aside all prejudices, and earnestly holding converse with nature and her undeviating laws, bending a willing mind to grasp all the blessings that must flow from the results of having pure seed, deep mellow soil, with all the organic substances that can be made from the stock, and every pound of offal vegetable matter created on the farm, should be returned to the soil, and a rich harvest must follow.

I now come to the time when corn should be harvested. There are two ways this is done. By husking and cribing, and cutting it up and shocking in the field. Economy tells me to husk the corn and have it safely taken care from all possible chances of getting wet. Oh, what an improvident, heedless, and miserable loss there is in the West, by not having proper care taken to secure all the produce the farmers have labored so assiduously to raise. I have seen farmers lose one thousand dollars on a crop of three thousand bushels, when one hundred dollars would have made him good, permanent cribs, from which a bushel of grain would not be wasted, and which would last twenty years.

The best grain house for safety, economy of labor and expense, is what I have recommended in my model farm arrangements, and from this position of loading in and out grain so free from much labor. I would build such a house as soon as time and means would permit. You can load up your teams over night, ready for an early start to market, and then you can in all kinds of weather prepare your grain for stock, by grinding and steaming what you may want for stock. There you can have a good place for all your seeds, kept in their pure state, ready at all times for special use. The utility of this grain house is so glaringly apparent to common sense, when once developed, that I feel assured that all farmers that have none, will do so when they have given it their true reflection. This can be put up in sections, as your wants and means require.

Now for saving your seed corn while you are husking. Take the baskets into the field with you, and all the stout, prominent, well ripened ears, that show evidence of an early growth, take these off with a few husks on them, then tie up when your boys have time in the stormy days, and hang them up in a warm place for winter, so that the germ shall not in any way receive the least injury; reflect for a moment; the germ in a grain of corn is not larger than a small grain of flax-seed, and is imbedded in the moist part of the berry; hence the great care in securing the firmest seed, and keep it in a dry place, where the frost cannot affect it, and no fears of a failure from the seed. I always took my seed from the middle of the cob, by shelling off the ends, the corn being more perfect.

There are two kinds of corn, the yellow and the white, and from these two there is a mixture of all colors, and for feeding stock of course just as good, and the largest crop I ever raised was of this kind. For stock feeding, I should plant this kind, watching the result as to the yield with the purer kinds.

No plants will hybridize as successfully as the corn, from its favorable position, and a very fruitful change will be made in one year, and I recommend experimental propagation of the different kinds in your small fields set apart for the propagation of seeds, for their more perfect excellence.

The pure white corn brings the best price for bread, and for manufacturing into starch. Some farmers delay harvesting their corn, until the freezing rains and snows come, costing double the amount of labor and suffering by frosted hands. It should be gathered in October and November, that the boys may be ready for school, an important item for their future welfare.

Friends, I have dwelt on this subject longer than I intended, but when I know that it is our country's greatest product, requiring much care and reflection by those who have it to raise, I feel that I cannot say too much in favor of the soil being made rich in all the substances that can possibly be obtained, and should be made deep and mellow, that the organs of the corn plant may receive all the strength from the soil that this culture can impart, so the farmers shall be richly rewarded for the extra pains they have taken, through the entire culture and saving of their farm products, so that when they have made out a true account showing the extra expense and the increase of production, it will give high encouragement for their future progress in the same line of action.

Under the better modes of husbandry, there is an inherent dignity in the occupation, that all should feel proud and full of emulation, discarding all disquietude and humiliation for the sun burnt complexion, or the dusty clothing for a season you may have to wear. For we have the gracious satisfaction of knowing it was the first special labor the Almighty enjoined upon mankind, and we know it is the foundation stepping stone for all other pursuits of life, giving aid and comfort to all branches of industry.

Being clothed with lasting blessings, that will carry the mind onward and upward, to that high eminence, affording rich pleasures in cultivating the vegetables, fruits and flowers, blending beauty and utility together, so energizing and healthful to bring out the better elements of mankind, that will prove a tower of strength in all relations of life.

These remarks I cheerfully submit to your candid and liberal consideration, hoping by due reflection you will have a desire to make a fair experimental trial, on the plans I have suggested, bearing in mind that corn cannot grow to make a full crop, without deep strong soil that will feed the plant from the time of its sprouting until it has put on its golden dress, showing it has all the excellent qualities and quantity that superior cultivation would warrant.

CHAPTER VI.

CATTLE RAISING.

The entire number of cattle in the twenty loyal States in 1865, was twelve million eight hundred and twenty-one thousand seven hundred and forty-one. Of this number there were four millions and upwards of cattle and oxen, and something over three millions of cows in the nine Western States, and a decrease of one million in all the States since 1864.

This has its origin from the heavy demands to supply, the army having taken a large number of cows away for beef, has and will stop the increase for several years to come. Hence, under all these existing facts, in regard to the falling off by such a large number of cattle in our country, it behooves the farmers of the west, the fountain-head of stock production, to take a fair comprehensive survey of all the available ground, for the purpose of bringing up an increase in number, and a large increase of weight and quality, so much needed in dollars, and for the reputation of the stock breeders of the west, where they have the best country on the top of our globe for raising stock.

Farmers of the west, I desire to have some candid talk with you on that important subject, controlling as it does more capital than any food product in our country, and having myself been a raiser of stock for twenty years in Illinois, preceeding the last ten.

Having been a close observer for ten years in Chicago of the condition of cattle brought here for market, knowing too the difference in value between a fat steer and an ordinary one, and the cause of this difference, I sensibly feel the need of farmers taking a higher stand on the plan of stock growing in the West.

When I look back thirty years ago, and follow my mind onward ten years, we can offer some little palliation for those raising stock at that time, who neglected their high moral duty, say nothing about their pecuniary interests, that was wasted so heedlessly in those gloomy years, from 1837 to 1847. For in that time I sold pork dressed for one cent per lb. and carriage twenty miles, and finding no market for beef at home, I shipped in barrels to New Orleans, and on return of sales I had to pay over charges on the entire shipment for freight, storage and commissions. Which would seem to blunt the sensibilities of our moral natures, that would warrant some feeble excuse for our neglects on taking care of our domestic animals at that time.

But my friends, when you have been getting from six to twelve cents per pound for beef and pork the past five years, it really seems—say nothing about any other feeling but the pocket—that all stock the farmer has, and especially beef, which is most effected by poor feeding and care, that you would with such high prices, feel stimulated to put on the last pound, and take the best possible care of your cattle from the time they are born until the time they are old enough for market. True, we have in the west many good cattle breeders, that send cattle to market that cannot be beaten in the world. But when we know there are a large number in the west raising cattle, but don't seem to have the care and pride so needful to warrant them to obtain these higher prices at the markets, and consequently have to lose twenty to forty dollars per head on their steers, which is grevious to themselves, and a discredit to the stock growing interests of the west.

Although not cultivating the soil for the past ten years, nevertheless, my mind has been uniformly true to the success and prosperity of the farmers of our country and especially of the west; and residing in Chicago, the great stock market of the country, being engaged the most of the time in the produce business, it is evident that my feelings and sight would be drawn to the condition of the products that have come to this market for the past ten years. And I am sorry to say no branch of the farmers industry has suffered so much as that of cattle; and now let me kindly ask every farmer in the west, why is this so? and what must be done to remedy the great evil that pervades quite a large portion of the west?

Having an inborn interest to see the cultivators of the soil prosper in all their labors in the most effectual manner, I will with my feeble pen, tell you from all the experience and observations I have had, what should be your course of action in order to accomplish these rich results.

The first duty the farmer has in raising stock, if in the summer, is to have plenty of good green food and water for his cattle, that is, rich prairie or tame grass, and be sure to have plenty of good water—I don't mean this thick muddy water, and little of that—I mean the running brook, or from the wells that can and must be made if you don't want your cattle to suffer, as many most horribly do, through the months of August and September for the want of water and food. The farmers should have plenty of wells in common on the prairies for their stock, saving the poor thirsting creatures from driving off miles to get water, and often disappointed at that. Although not human, they are your domestic animals, subject to innate sufferings for the want of food and water same as the human species. Don't the farmers keep these animals for the rich food they so abundantly furnish you? Even if you furnish the cows with good pure water and plenty of sweet rich food, they will supply you with the greatest luxuries in the rich milk, cream, and the greatest of all, that high flavored yellow butter, being made rich in sugar and other essential properties from the pure sweet water; and the food should be from the rich grasses; and when they become exhausted in their season, have on hand, the best of all, the sown corn that you can give daily to your cows, which is the true secret of having good full grown fat stock. It is an unmistakable fact that nothing of the animal kind that you don't require to labor, should ever lose a pound of flesh for the want of good care and plenty of food. This is wanted from the farmers, and none can fail to see it, if he will take one stormy day when the mind is at rest, and give his mature reflection on the subject, and the favorable effects of your care and attention paid to your cattle through the summer, will incite you onward to the utmost care through the bleak winter storms so fatal to a large loss by shrinkage, occasioned by short feed and the exposure to the sleeting, freezing rains that come during winter, without shelter on the prairies, must create a great loss and even death to many valuable creatures if they could have had proper care; and I know to my regret the truth of this last assertion, for I increased my stock one winter and did not enlarge my sheltering capacity to cover them all, and the most severe sleeting, freezing storm came, the last of Febuary, and the steers drove out the cows from the shelter, and I lost three valuable cows, and more were injured: that was a fatal storm for Illinois.

Having somewhat experienced these fatal scenes in the early times of my farming, I feel the more sensitive to have the farmers make ample room to give protection for all their stock, and this can only be done by a will and determination to have these things all in readiness. For the safety of your entire stock, it is better to have little to much than not enough, for you will soon want all you have and need more; it is a good sign to see farmers always ahead on room and food for their animals.

If a farmer has various grades of cattle, from calves up, he should have three apartments—one for his grown steers and oxen, one for his cows and spring calves, and one for his yearlings and two-year-olds. This will save much trouble and loss by preserving the weaker from the tyranny of the stronger, wounds often being inflicted where they are all together. If you have any malicious animals which want to be continually fighting, have a small place to put these by themselves until they can be quiet. We have all seen the evil arising from the neglect of this practice, and have suffered thereby.

For economy and utility, I recommend troughs, for feeding all cattle according to their size. By this plan they will save and eat all; whereas if you put the food on the ground, and especially in a wet time, one half will be lost. In each trough there should also be placed a small salt box.

Farmers who have a start in raising cattle and hogs, should provide themselves with feed grinding machines, which can be readily obtained. These will pay all expenses the first year. All grains should be ground for full feeding or fattening cattle, saving as it does, one third the food, besides putting on fat much faster.

If your stock are from the calf up, you want a ton of hay or good corn fodder, cut up, or a ton of good oat or barley straw, well saved in good ricks, that you can cut with your cutters, and at times take a barrel and make some brine and sprinkle it over your straw and hay as you feed it out in dry weather. I think one ton of this will keep your cattle on an average for the winter, but it is a good plan to leave some to spare.

O, what a pleasure to the farmer who has his stock all under good shelter, where the winds cannot come through the yard fences, as we often see in the country, creating much suffering among your cattle, and severe loss to yourselves.

It is the duty of every farming township, especially those under the Organization Culture, to establish rules by consent to restrain all seed animals from running at large, from the fact that many worthless animals of the cattle and hog species are in the Spring straying over the entire farming districts. Often these scrubs will make a cross on the best breeds, destroying the effects of having better stock. No farmer would object to such a just and feasible law, advancing the interests of all who are raising stock. I would that farmers who are not able to own the best breeding bulls, club together and purchase such as they may want to serve their cows, and in a few years, any of these farmers will be able to have their own if they desire. Carry this essential measure out throughout the West, and in five years twenty-five per cent. will be added to the value of the cattle, besides the improvement in their constitutional qualities to sustain them onward to a higher state of perfection. These important features should sink deep in the minds of the farmers of the West, that will impel them to make the trial. It is available, and none should doubt the rich results that would follow such an enterprise.

Much importance is attached to the care you give your young stock up to the time of their being two years old. For if they become stunted during that time, they can never overcome it, and just in proportion will their weight and quality be cut short. Hence the utmost care is requisite to see that they have plenty of the right kind of food, and warm shelter in winter to keep them growing in bone and flesh. For increasing the bone, which is of the most importance, I would feed them with ground oats, barley or rye. These contain fibrous matter that will enlarge the bones, so essential to all animal natures.

If farmers wish to be successful in cultivating their soil, they should as fast as they get their farms open, commence raising stock; it is a lasting source of wealth.

If you are in any of the western states, you should raise some cattle, if the corn don't grow as large, you are in a fine location for the dairy; you should have choice cows and raise some stock, and make all the choice butter you can. These cattle materially enrich your soil from the manures they will make, which is essential to keep your soil supplied with rich food for your succeeding crops.

Certainly the farm looks more cheerful with cattle on it; how pleasant to the sight, and warm to the feeling to see more or less cattle attached to the farm, and with proper care and attention they will pay a large interest from the investment, but without you have a taste for cattle, and will not take good care of them from the start, you had better let them alone.

Every farmer raising stock should according to his capacity make arrangements to fatten so many head every year, if they are four years old tney should weigh sixteen hundred, but to do this they must have been tended well during these four years, in having plenty of good grazing and well salted in the summer, and strong feed in the winter, so if you have only a few of them they will always, under any state of the market, bring you a good price.

It is an evident prevailing fact that cannot be disputed, that the connection between the cultivation of the soil and breeding and rearing stock, are inseparable. Hence the great important interest of farmers should be to study their climate, soil and taste for the kind of stock they would like to raise ; and for the sake of success, he should raise that kind that will be the most profitable in the end. Under these facts, he must reconcile his desires with the facilities he has before him, and devote his best energies to produce the rich results of cultivating his lands with products in vegetable and animal, that will yield the largest profits for the most judicious amount of labor rendered. Hence it would seem advisable for the farmers of the Northern part of Illinois, Wisconsin, Minnesota, and the Northern half of Iowa, to raise sheep, horses, and as far as possible cattle, through the influence and large income from the dairy, having the natural advantages of climate, soil and water, which the cows must have to make good butter and cheese, you will notice more fully in my essay on the dairy. And there are some localities in the other Western states, that are adapted to the dairy business.

But when you settle on these rich level prairies and timber, you should devote your energies to raising neat cattle most exclusively, for these rich soils, if cultivated on a subsoil basis, will produce one hundred bushels of corn per acre and two or three tons of Timothy to the acre, and clover as a legal tender to the success of good farming. Who can doubt, with good stock and proper care, but those who have taste for the stock growing business, will make fortunes from the capital invested.

Farmers in proportion to their farms and facilities for growing stock, should set apart such a number as the age will permit, and put them under the best keeping, especially the last year, that will make them first class beeves, and put them into market when they are needed for their better qualities. Even if your farm and means are small, a half dozen of choice fat steers will bring you from six to nine hundred dollars; to those who may think this a large estimate, can be witnessed at the Chicago market frequently, and these results are obtained on all well developed cattle, with good care taken from the first until they are four years old, and they cost no more than cattle that don't bring more than one half that money; for when a creature is full tended he cannot consume as much food. And why will not farmers in general adopt this method of raising their stock, so to increase largely the weight of their pockets, and having the reputation of doing full justice to their domestic animals, so requisite to elevate upward all who will clothe themselves with the true knowledge of cultivating the soil, and raising their stock in accordance with the laws of nature.

Exemplifying the great living truths, that just in proportion will you take care of your stock in all that will give aid to strengthen the vital system of your animals in proper food, pure water and shelter, and the physical and chemical laws at all times, most urgently require; and so with all the vegetable plants, the soil must be supplied with the proper organic food that their natural constitution require to give them their true growth, full of rich vitality, which by the wisdom of man all animals adapted to his wants, will all humanity be benefited, and the husbandman who has accomplished these high duties will receive his lasting rewards.

CHAPTER VII.

WHEAT CULTURE.

The wheat plant has the largest consumption by the human family in bread, than any other cereal grain, and much time and labor has been expended by the most scientific minds in all agricultural countries, in searching out by chemical analysis the composition of soils most available in their natural state, and with much care in adjusting the essential organic constituent substances soils must have as food, in order to insure a good crop of wheat.

I can look back with feelings of regret when I was cultivating the soil of Illinois at the careless and indifferent manner we tended the soil for wheat culture, and the ignorance that prevailed among the farmers, throughout the west, in not securing their grain immemediately after harvest, instead of leaving it in the shock, exposed to rains and bleaching sun, destroying the qualities of the grain for seed or good bread. It is true there has been improvements made by some in the wheat culture, but there are vast improvements to be carried out in preparing the soil with the elements necessary to give strength and vigor to the plant, to insure a good harvest. Therefore rotation of plants in their most available order, and deep cultivation of the soil, for all purposes, I make a speciality, to insure successful farming. By this rotation of culture, you have continually an acquisition, by the rich strength you have from the clover to fallow down as often as you think beneficial. And here let me say, that by your regular changing, you renew your soil with food, and by plowing under all the vegetable substances on your land as soon as your grain is off, you retain much that would be lost if suffered to lay over until spring. Hence, it is of the utmost importance to the farmers, to adopt this plan of cultivating their farms as soon as possible, that they may have their rewards for their better culture.

When we know there are fifteen hundred pounds of wheat and three thousand pounds of straw from an acre, it must be apparent to every reflecting farmer, that the soil producing this amount of vegetable substance, must have exhausted a large portion of its organic elements that it had on hand, and what it received from the dews and rains while growing. And further reflection will convince those cultivating the soil, that they must make an equivalent deposit if they expect their drafts to be honored by their mother earth in the next twelve months. And how are they to do this without they return all the offal arising from the straw being made into manure or spread in its raw state over some of the land and ploughed under in the fall; the stubble of all the cereals should be turned under as soon as possible; it costs no more in the end.

In my remarks on rearing cattle, I make a special statement that no farmer can prosper well without keeping some animal stock; and I think it is a duty they owe to themselves, and to the prosperity of the country, to cultivate that kind to which their soil and climate is best adapted to secure success in the keeping of stock.

The rotation of crops is a simple undertaking; but to give the plants their true relative position when you make these changes, requires care and discretion to have each kind follow that which will render the strongest support for all the plants you desire to cultivate on your farm in rotation. Hence, if you want to raise wheat, corn, oats and rye, which are the most substantial crops cultivated, I would commence my rotation crops by sowing clover with the fall wheat, or in the spring with wheat or oats; or you can sow it in the fall or spring with rye. Now those who will adopt this clover culture in part for fertilizing the soil, will find it the best *legal tender* instituted, paying the largest interest; and no farmer should refuse to invest. If you seed down clover in the Fall, I would prefer a rye or an oat lay, and plow it well under, ten inches deep. If you cannot obtain seed of summer rye, you can sow spring wheat or oats, and harrow your ground well, and then sow fourteen pounds of clover seed to the acre and take a fine brush and put it in well. If in a dry time, roll it down well. If wheat, put on two bushels, if oats, put on four bushels per acre. Rich soil will bear heavy seeding, the crop will ripen up the sooner and be less liable to fall down. Sow as early as possible; in the Fall, take what land you have had in oats or rye, and plow it up, turning the stubble under about ten inches, and harrow it well before seeding. Drill your wheat in, then sow your clover seed, and with your roller compress the soil; and if you have any high ground on the piece, after the ground has frozen up hard, put on some coarse straw manure, which and serve to protect the crop from too hard freezing, and enrich the soil, feed the grain and clover plants, and thereby ensure a good crop.

By crossing three kinds of grain, say wheat, corn and oats, or change the wheat or oats for rye, you will have a clover lay every year after three years, to turn over, making your soil full of new mold, which with a judicious management in saving and applying all the manures, in the most needful places, keeping all the stock you can fatten well at the youngest age, the mind's eye must be weak indeed that cannot see the great changes that will follow the farmers who adopt this course of cultivating their farms, strictly on the rotation and deep plowing principle, using every available means to make all the manures you can to enrich the soil.

The selection of seed—Winter or Spring—as your soil most requires, is an object that farmers should attentively look at, seeking after that seed which is full of life and strength as capable of producing the most excellent wheat, having all the rich elements of starch, sugar and gluten, that must enhance the value for flouring purposes. In this procedure lies the profits of raising wheat.

Drilling wheat is far preferable to broad-cast sowing, placing the grain at a regular depth, all having the same covering, being well secured against freezing out, as the soil is continually working into the drilled furrows, thereby protecting the roots, so vital to the plants' existence, through the winter; whereas by the broad-cast seeding, a considerable portion of the seed is hardly covered and in such an exposed condition as to leave it in danger of destruction, or crippled so that the plant, from the want of nourishment, will stool out one foot high, and the product of such, in a shrunk condition, will lower the value of your crop ten to twenty cents per bushel. Hence the great importance of drilling wheat, for profit and reputation of good culture.

The several kinds I am most familiar with are the White Winter Blue Stem, will hold its white complexion and fairness in the southern half of Illinois, part of Indiana and Ohio, all of Kentucky and quite a large part of Missouri, also in much of the dry burr oak openings of Michigan; the May White Winter, is a strong hardy wheat, making excellent flour and is earnestly sought after by the millers, and can be well cultivated in any soil or climate suitable for producing White Winter wheat. I would recommend this wheat to growers, as it ripens up in June, saving the dangers of rust so fatal at times in some localities, and on this account wheat in all the Western States should be sown from the 10th to the 12th of September, having a good start, and if a late warm fall and your wheat is having a luxuriant growth, put on your calves and let them take off some of the top blades, as too much growth in the fall will in a warm wet spring be liable to scald the roots; in that case after the heavy freezing is over, put on a light harrow and scratch off the the dead covering and it will have new life and vigor at once, and will hasten the plant forward so essential for an early harvest.

Any farmer who don't feel sure to make this trial in full, I would advise him to try some, and by this experiment he will learn the facts as they are, and by this find out much that will enrich his pockets and save many hard days labor.

There is a new White Winter wheat called the Tapahannock, and is held to be a choice hardy wheat. I have no personal knowledge of its superior qualities. It is raised in Southern Illinois, and I would advise farmers to try it. There is also a Red May Wheat, both winter and spring, sound and will grow where all the red wheats will, and is being cultivated quite extensively throughout the west.

So far as I am acquainted, and from all I can learn from the cultivators and millers for the spring qualities, I will mention the justly celebrated Rio Grande when found in its purity, will grow well on soil that has a full share of lime and other constituents that will support the plants, as their nature require until harvest.

The miller can make choice flour from such wheat, full of starch and glutenous properties, and is very desirable for family use. Oh ! how much importance there is in the farmers raising pure seed, and with care and little pains taken in sowing such, and keeping it pure from all mixture when they thresh their grain. All that is wanting in this matter is active reflection and a will to carry their sober second thoughts out to have pure seed ; and all such tending efforts will add much wealth and comfort to the farmer who adopts this mode of culture.

There is also the Tea Wheat, having high claims for its rich producing qualities, and the millers are anxious to procure it as being full of the rich qualities that make good flour. When grown from pure seed it will always rank among the first of spring wheats, and I strongly recommend this wheat to the farmers of the west ; and should, from its large size, have on strong land, two bushels to the acre, which will aid an early harvest.

Then the next seed I am most familiar with by cultivation is the Soft Shell Siberian, very fair, bright red, and in many places entirely run out by its mixture, which can be reclaimed by propagation. It is true the stem is tender, but with two bushels of seed on the acre on good dry land from a clover lay, thirty to forty bushels per acre may be raised, and will sell well in any market if it is pure Siberian.

In the Western states, I know from observation, the farmers have in their long culture of corn and wheat, without any change or rest, often burnt up the stubbles, preventing any visible organic substance returning to the soil, so essential to give life and strength to the next crop. By this practice we see the lamentable results of twelve bushels to the acre; and this state of things is certain to continue as long as the farmers adhere to their old stereotyped habits of culture, and they cannot hope to make any improvements in raising the average on the product of wheat, so beneficial to themselves and the whole people.

Now in all kindness let me say to you, what I know by all the facts of practical experience, observation and study—do contend with all the power my mind is able to bear—to press home these important facts to the farmers—that they may hold converse with their better judgment, in their quiet moments of reflection, that will excite their physical powers, and join in one united voice with their fellow farmers in their townships, and form clubs, with a chairman and secretary, and go to work immediately and open a discussion for the promulgation and substitution of a perpetual, well-regulated, established system of planting and sowing by rotation of all the leading plants they desire to cultivate, from the most efficient knowledge of what their soil and climate is by nature best adapted to grow.

Then, with these rotations of crops, after two years, by cultivation of the clover, after the product of grain, furnishing the strong elements of lime, and other constituents, drawing and extracting from the elements of air and water, much of the lactescent fluids that abound in the composition of animals and plants, which must be returned to the soil.

The more I study over the culture and products of our country, and especially the west where I am most familiar, the more I see the necessity of the farmers taking more efficient and higher views in the culture of wheat, that the country may witness a higher average than was made in the year of 1864.

For we find in the reports from Washington, the the low average of twelve bushels to the acre, from this take one and a half bushels for seed, and we have ten and a half bushels left per acre as an increase, with this state of facts I know from my own experience, taking all the expenses of culture one half of the cultivators must have lost money on their wheat culture for that year.

Now my friends let me say to you that I am well aware that there is some farmers who understand how to cultivate wheat, but without any disrespect, where there is one who does, there are twenty who do not, and the evidence of this low average warrants this conclusion; I know the rust, the most fatal and to some extent, unavoidable fatal affection that can happen it. And some land is put into wheat that is too poor and destitute of life to support the weakest plant cultivated, much less to sustain the most requiring and difficult plant known to farmers. I am truly astonished to see wheat sown upon such soil when labor is entirely lost to the worthy laborer who should look more to his interest and lift the credit of raising wheat to a high standard.

Now, what is wanted most to obviate these unavoidable results, is one united effort and an uprising of the farmers to a sense of their just duties, in wheat culture, that they may know that it requires a deep mellow soil of sand and clay loam supplied with the organic vegetable elements substituted by all possible means the farmer has, in returning all offal vegetation in whatever form to the soil before plowing the same, and at all times as fast as it accumulates, to save wastage by the exposure to evaporation. Then with a judicious management of your rotations of crops as I have before stated, and strict care to have the pure seeds, who can doubt the results of this mode of cultivating wheat. And who will doubt the fact that an average of twenty bushels per acre can be grown in the nine Western states, which in 1864, returned one hundred and twenty-three millions of bushels of wheat, grown on ten millions of acres of land, making a fraction over twelve bushels per acre.

And who, I repeat again, can doubt that, with improved culture, twenty bushels per acre can be raised, which will add to these nine Western states as follows: Estimated account of wheat grown in nine Western states, say in 1869, when the farmers will be prepared to raise twenty bushels per acre on ten millions of acres of land, producing a total of two hundred millions of bushels. Deduct a hundred and twenty-three millions as the product of 1864, and we have a total increase in the production of seventy-seven millions of bushels for 1869.

This can be demonstrated. In fact, with proper care and exertion by the farmer, without much extra labor, only attend to all the features that I have laid down, in restoring the soil to full vigorous strength, with food that is afforded to the farmers for this special purpose, so as to give effect to all their labors, and attending faithfully to all the requirements as they may arise from time to time.

When your wheat is ready for harvest, make all preparation to have it put up as soon as possible. Do not stop at a little expense in employing plenty of hands, which you can almost always find in the towns and villages in the country.

Reaping and heading are both good in their place. For the early harvest, the reaper is preferable, because if the crop is a little green, you can save it well in the shock, while the header must wait until your grain is fully ripe, so as you can save it in the stack. For wheat that is dead ripe, they render excellent service, and farmers raising large quantities of wheat, should have them in their neighborhood ready for their last harvesting. Utility and economy should dictate this.

Always get the best machines in the country; they can be readily found in the West. I don't see many of the ten-feet reapers I cut my grain with. I could average twenty acres per day. They were the best in the country at that time.

Much importance rests upon the farmers in having their grain stacked or ricked. Ricking I think is the best, because you can put more into the ricks, and more safely secured from the weather; after three days good weather I would put a team stacking grain, and every day you do this, you have so much secured from the bleaching rains that happen, and well do I remember leaving my grain out, sixty acres of choice White Winter, and the rain set in and I lost one half my crop by its growing, I am sorry to say I was not alone, and I see many farmers continue the same practice. Now farmers you can see at once this is a very important item, for you have expended much labor and money on your grain, in fact all you can spend, but to take care of it; hence no farmer should let it remain in the field one day after it is ready to put up, don't stop to go fishing or hunting until you have your grain, and especially wheat secure.

Now friends before closing this subject on wheat culture, let me suggest to you a plan for successfully saving your grain at all times in the rick, first get some pine boards as long as you may want to cut in two, so they will be as long as the roof of your ricks are deep, and get some two-by-six joist and make sections in length to suit your taste on the side of your rick, by nailing boards on to the joist, and then put on a good batting to make them water tight, by having at the connection of these sections a batting to lap over on the other, so water cannot get through; have these made already to use when you commence ricking, that if a shower overtakes you before you finish a rick, you have a complete shelter for your wheat, by having a few braces ready made out of joist to hold the roof, that you can put up a temporary shelter over your grain for the night, so that in the morning your rick of wheat as it is partially finished, is perfectly dry, affording much pleasure by not having to take off the wet wheat, as you and I have done, many times, if you are an old farmer.

You will see the use of hooks and staples to hold these sections at the top and bottom. To keep all the water out of the ridge pole, you can make a cap out of two boards, that will surely prevent any water from getting on your wheat.

It is essential to make your wheat saving complete, to have your beds for laying your grain on raised up from the damp ground one foot, by having blocks enough set on the ground to hold your flooring for your wheat; reflection will prompt you to do this, and save more than it cost you the first year, and the poultry will live on the waste grain that may drop in your stack yard. The fruits of this little expense are rich and (good many in hill) as the farmer would say, first when you come to thresh your grain sooner or later, instead of having to pitch off much that is bleached and partly rotten all over the roof of your ricks, say nothing, as I have had wet holes down through them and more or less spoiled, and the worst of it, many rotten grains remain unavoidably in the wheat that you have to lose, on selling, from five to twenty cents per bushel.

Now these are not all the benefits and blessings that these sections of shedding will render you, for when you have done threshing your grain, which is often the case before winter sets in, you can most carefully remove them to your stock yard, where you can place them on a frame which you should have in readiness to shelter your calves and cows from the wintry blasts, and keep them warm. Humanity and economy require this at your hands.

In addition to this, to make your grain in the rick, either reaped or headed, safe, I have conceived a plan which is very feasible, and in all cases, should be adopted. It is simply to make some slat tubings twelve inches square, and place them through the ricks as close as may seem advisable, running them crosswise, or it may seem wise to run one twelve inches square lengthwise. These tubings must possess facilities for drying, and prevent the grain in a damp time from being musty, which is so often the case in wet weather. When the wind is dry, shut up the opposite side of the tubing, and the wind penetrating through the ricks, it must prove beneficial to the wheat. The experiment is worth trying, and I hope the farmers of the West will give my remarks on wheat culture, although somewhat lengthy, an impartial reading, and give the leading suggestions a fair experimental trial, hoping they may fulfil their most sanguine expectations, so that a larger harvest may reward their extra labors adding more honor to agriculture in the West, causing it to take a march forward toward that high position where the strongest hopes of our country are sure to dwell.

CHAPTER VIII.

HOG CULTURE.

From the statistics of 1865, we find there were in the twenty-one loyal states thirteen millions, seventy thousand, eight hundred and eighty-seven hogs, being a decrease from 1864 of three millions seventy-seven thousand eight hundred and twenty-five, and out of this number in the twenty-one states, there was raised in nine western states nine millions, one hundred and eighty-three thousand, seven hundred and seventy-two, which clearly shows that the west is the most available place for raising stock, and especially hogs and cattle; but my friends, when we see such a decrease in number in 1865, it will be for the farmers to ask themselves how they will make up this decrease in number and increase in weight and quality so desirable.

From my experience and observations, I think there is no one product in proportion to the capital invested, that a greater improvement can be made than on the hog product of our country—and of course I mean the west.

The first thing the farmers have to do to realize this result, is to improve their breeds, and in doing that, they will have a desire to take better care of them; the best breeds in our country at this time is the Chester County Whites, the Suffolk and the Berkshire, they all have good qualities for making heavy pork ; when I was farming I raised the imported Berkshire and Leicestershire, by crossing them, and raised fine large hogs from them, and could make them weigh from four to five hundred pounds at fifteen to eighteen months old.

The Chester White and Suffolk have fattening qualities over any breeds, possessing the capacity to put on more weight at a given age than any yet before the farmers. But from my observation, I think the Berkshire pork has more solidity than any I have seen, and I would recommend a cross of the Chester White and Suffolk with the Berkshire; and I think they would do well together by continually changing them. There should be a cross either in the male or female going forward yearly, which is the only way farmers can keep up their breeds. Large farmers can keep the different kinds, while small farmers can exchange or purchase, so as to keep their stock in the right order for producing the most meat.

The best way for keeping and feeding hogs in the West is known and practised only by very few farmers, and they seem to be confined to certain neighborhoods. I am surprised that the better grades of stock, and better ways of taking care of it, are not more universally chosen and adopted.

From my own experience and observation of the hogs as they come to Chicago market, and notice their age, and see the great difference there is in their weight and fatness, I am convinced that many neglect to adopt the right plan for feeding hogs; and to those who sell their hogs in such a condition, and have not adopted the better plan, I would kindly say—try the experiment.

Build your hog pen large enough to hold all your hogs and pigs, so that when the cold, sleety, freezing weather comes on in the fall, you will have them comfortable to fatten, and your stock hogs and breeding sows so situated as to thrive and grow onward in size rapidly.

To do well, you want four partition pens—one for your fattening hogs, one for your breeding sows, one for your stock hogs, and one for your second size hogs which you desire to fatten for the spring market. This plan, if you are raising many hogs, will pay you well.

There are many plans of building hog pens, and some may think any way will do. I acted somewhat upon that idea when I first came West, to be in the fashion; but I found that hogs needed care and comfort, as they did in Maine, if I expected to make any thing by them. Good hog pens can be made with shed roof, twelve to fourteen feet wide, five or six feet high in front, and three and a half feet in the rear, and as large as you may desire for all your hogs. Have your pen raised up one foot from the ground to keep rats out; have floor joists two by six inches; studding two by four; tight weather boarding to keep out the rain and snow. Leaking pens create a wetness if suffered to remain in the pen, will give hogs the mange, and otherwise affect their healthy growth. Eight hogs need a sixteen feet pen for fattening. Your pens for breeding, to give room, should be five feet wide to hold one, which is essential while they are bearing their young. Your stock hogs during the winter should be separated according to size, in pens from ten to fifteen, which will prevent their fighting, and give them a chance to do well, by each having his own share of the food with the same room.

There should be slide doors in the rear side to let hogs out, and at the top of this slide it will be well to have narrow windows, and at the other front where you feed have also slide windows, that you may close up or leave open as to the weather, to give plenty of ventilation, so essential to all animal life, even the hog that furnish such fine bacon, delicious hams and pure white lard, that no other animal can furnish you. These pens should incline to the front to keep the wet at the trought, and one end of each pen should be assigned for the hogs to use in, and they will occupy it when needed that you can remove at leisure ; any farmer can see the utility of this; there should be a low guard put down in your pens to hold the litter where the hogs sleep.

This pen will cost fifty to sixty cents all complete per lineal foot, and the experiment of having such a pen over the wasteful habit of feeding on the wet frozen ground, will pay the cost of building the first year, and those who don't quite see it in that light, let me kindly remind them of the facts as they have existed for the past thirty years more or less, to my certain knowledge in the west, that instead of these dry pens in the fall and winter to shelter and feed hogs in, they have been suffered as a general thing to have their pens by a water run, to fatten their hogs in, and in the fore part of the fall when the rains fill up the creek it seems to do very well, but when freezing time comes, I have seen corn thrown into these pens, and the hogs while trying to eat the corn would get well coated with mud frozen on their limbs.

To correct their stomachs, which at times become debilitated and diseased for the want of proper food, and right here, I would ask any farmer of fair reflection, or medical man, if they don't think all this so-called hog cholera and trichenia has not been occasioned, and had their origin from the severe exposure of the hogs, in not having suitable food, water and shelter, and we have cause to know that these animals, many of them, have suffered severely in the distillery pens, having nothing to eat but the offal slops at times, from poor miserable rotten corn, and remaining in those pens exposed to the hot sun would seem to be impossible that they could live, and then taking the exposure of keeping them in pens all winter without shelter, freezing at times even unto death, and no proper food nor medicine to stop and check the disease these extreme sufferings would inflict upon them all, would warrant the probability of such animals having something that would resemble cholera and the trichenia, that a number of medical men took council over a year ago, which I am happy to learn no further investigation has been required from them on the subject as far as the trichenia is concerned, I have no apprehension that they will be needed any more. Hence my advise to the farmers is, to have their hog-pens, and give them plenty of food, and in the spring sow peas and oats together, as I have directed in another place, and keep no more than what you can feed full from the time they are weaned until they are ready for market, and the result will pay richly for all the extra trouble and expense of building hog-pens, and other labor rendered. And I have seen these poor dumb animals that make such clean white food for the human family, not being able to get half what they needed and they would all go to their place of sleeping in this condition in the fence corner, often times without any cover on them, and they would pile up and the largest and strongest would over-lay many others, causing much distress on the smallest and even death, that would make loss enough in one week to build such pens as I have recommended, say nothing of the moral obligation man is under to protect his domestic animals, he holds by right of subjugation.

Now in addition to pens for comfort I come to the better plans and means for feeding hogs, that I know from my own experience, that by these pens, and having food ground and steamed in kettles, and plenty given regular three times per day, will soon as it is eaten, go into active service to put on flesh, if the right breed of hogs, two pounds per day, and not take any more grain in the end. This is the true way for keeping and fattening hogs, and the sooner all the farmers adopt them, the better it will be for themselves, and more wealth to the country.

For fattening hogs, one bushel of ground corn, well steamed into the substance of pudding with a little salt stirred in after being cooked will feed seven hogs, and give them at the same time some liquid slop made from oats or barley mashed up, and have it stand until it is a little sour, will add much to the appetite and secure strong vigorous growth, with plenty of bituminous coal or charcoal kept in their pens that they can eat daily as they may want.

Much caution is required to take proper care of sows while breeding. A sow that is one year old when she has her first litter in the spring, will bear another in September, making part of your stock hogs fourteen and seventeen to eighteen months old, which is a good age, and if well tended, they will weigh from four to five hundred pounds each, and perhaps more.

As soon as your pigs are six weeks old, wean them and put them in pens by themselves; give them first boiled milk with a small quantity of corn and rye meal with a little salt in it. If they get the scours, take crust of bread, burn and pulverize it and put it into their food; this will set them right. Feed them three times a day, and do not give them too much at a time. Wash them well once a week, and increase the quantity of their food gradually. Near the time that your sows will have pigs, give them a little meat to quiet their carniverous appetite so voracious at that time. Watch the growth of the vigorous and most prominent pigs, both male and female, and when they are weaned, put them in pens by themselves, and sell them to those who need them to improve the stock of the country. It is just as cheap to keep the best as the poorest. All the pigs you don't want for seed, alter them one week after you wean them. I would wash the breeding sows occasionally with soap suds, using a coarse brush with a handle on it. This will give life and good health to them to rear their young, adding much to your interest as a stock grower.

In one year, if farmers will adopt this plan in taking care of their hogs, we shall, on the nine millions of hogs, if the farmers will have as many, in the nine Western states in 1868, making an increase of fifty pounds per hog, would give a gain of twenty-two millions and five hundred dollars, which would be a fine increase. I base this conclusion upon facts under my own observation and experience, and feel assured if my suggestions are carried out as per programme, they will be fully realized by every farmer in proportion to the number of his hogs. Try the experiment in your township organizations, and prove the assurance that the result will be accomplished.

My motto is, never let any stock go back for one day, if they are in good health, for want of plenty of food. Espouse this principle and rigidly carry it out, and success and prosperity must attend all your efforts in cultivating your soil and rearing your stock. If your means are small, your progress will be rapid, and in a few years, with the blessings of good health, you will be registered one of the benefactors of your country. And may you be the witness to prove my prediction.

CHAPTER IX.

RYE CULTURE.

This grain is not fully appreciated by the farmers of the west, especially those raising stock for the dairy. There is no grain cultivated affording so much nutritious pasturage as the rye. You can sow it on your oat lay the first of August, one and a half bushels per acre, and the first of September you can turn your calves on it, and you can see them grow, and by the middle of September you can let your milch cows on it, and you can see them increase in milk, and choice butter will be the result.

We would advise the farmers having stock, to put it in their corn just as soon as it is ripe in the fall, with a fine tooth cultivator, and as soon as you have your first piece of corn harvested, put your cattle in that field and they will have the richest food that can be supplied to animals, and as soon as the flush of the corn is eaten off they will have the rye to graze on in the winter, when the ground is dry and hard; never suffer your stock in the fields when the ground is soft, by this, your soil will loose much of its organic substance by disturbing the quiet rest nature designed it should have through one half the year.

In my last years of cultivating the soil, I could not do without my large rye field, and the rich pleasure I had in seeing my young stock and cows feed on that rye is not erased from my mind yet, and those who have tried it will bear evidence to the fact I have stated. This in your corn stubble you can plow under in the spring, affording extra food for your next crop of oats or spring wheat with your clover which would be the best lay you could have for it; all this food for your cattle with only the cost of the rye and sowing, it is the most hardy plant the farmer has to cultivate. I never have seen a crop of rye frozen out.

Rye will do well in Northern latitudes, including the middle and Western states. The best soil is a dry sandy loam, and all friable soils; but for family use, it should grow on a sandy soil, where lime more or less exists. From such a soil you can obtain the quality that will furnish the rich meal which is so essential to mix with your pure white or yellow corn, to make that justly celebrated rye and Indian bread, that New England people can lay to without feelings of regret.

And the more this bread is used as food for the human family, the fewer dyspeptic, chronic, diseased subjects we shall have in our country. Hence I strongly recommend the culture of rye, and believe it is possessed of all the advantages attributed to it, and for all purposes is equal to any of the cereal grains.

The time for cutting is when the berry is full in the dough, making the flour whiter and the straw affording substance for chopping up to mix with grain for horses and cattle, when mashed up, serving to accumulate the rich manures that farmers must have on their soil in some way yearly to keep up that state of culture that will produce a full harvest of all plants the farmer may want to grow.

These remarks on the culture of rye, I hope the farmers that have not had the practical experience of the utility of this crop, will make a trial as I have directed, with all their better judgment, and I am sure the result will give full satisfaction, add to your wealth, and the rich blessings it will afford to those who have not the means to raise it, being devoted to other occupations of life, will say you have done well for us. And we will advise you to keep on doing so.

CHAPTER X.

SHEEP CULTURE.

We find by the reports for 1865, there were in twenty-one Northern and Western States, twenty-eight millions six hundred and forty-seven thousand, two hundred and sixty-nine sheep, being an increase of four millions, three hundred thousand, eight hundred and seventy-eight sheep over 1864.

But with this increase, the demand for wool is good, and especially the long wools for warp in satinet cloths for which cotton was used before the war and there are a number of enterprising manufacturers in Massachusetts who have commenced the manufacture of worsted dress goods, worsted braids, and other trimmings, which require wool having a long fibre. Not being able to find it in our country, they have had to go to Canada to purchase, at sixty-five to seventy cents per pound, currency.

These long wools are sought after in Europe as well as in our country, from the fact that they can comb long wool by machinery, making these wools greatly in demand, while we have plenty of the finer grades.

Hence the importance of making strong exertions to raise the long wool sheep, such as the Leicester,

Yorkshire and the Cotswold. The wool from these sheep comes in competition by making fabrics of the imitation of the Alpaca, and no doubt will continue. In addition to this, the production of mutton and lambs which at the present time of scarcity of neat cattle will enhance the value of these larger grades of sheep, and I know the meat from these sheep and lambs is better flavored, and with the abundance of rich food we have in the west, would make these grades very valuable for their fleece, being elastic and good length, from the plenty of strong feeding, and the carcase dressed would weigh one hundred pounds; and I appeal to the western farmer as evidence to the fact that the lambs have a thrifty growth, and make excellent healthy meat for summer use, especially after the green pea makes its appearance.

Therefore these three important points—wool, mutton and lambs—which has rendered sheep culture so very valuable to the English farmer, with great profits to their manufacturers, giving them a large and almost exclusive control of the entire market of the world, for the manufacture of the imitation Alpaca dress goods, which can be made quite as remunerative in this country, as the trial has abundantly proven.

In reference to the profits of the Cotswold and Leicester, I quote a statement made by Mr. G. C. Rice, of Conn., to the Agricultural committee, of seven lambs dropped the 1st of February 1865, and sold them to the butcher on the 15th of May for $42.75 cents, and he sold three of them for stock for $22; and these five that were dropped later, he sold in the middle of July for $24 24; these were the produce of nine ewes. He also sold seventy and a half pounds of wool for 40 cents per pound unwashed, $28 20. Total $118 19. This with the cheapness of food in the west would have paid equally as well if not more by shipping it to eastern states.

My experience in raising sheep at an early day in the state of Maine, when all farmers raised more or less, I can vividly recall the pleasant scenes of sheep washing in those clear brooks, with nothing to disturb but the limber speckled trout taking their flight from us. And when I reflect also on the quiet manner in which I could lay them on the bench and take their fleeces off without even a murmur, I am not surprised at the rich emblematical comparison of the poet, as to their remarkable innocence. And under all circumstances, if the farmer has dry table lands, and any taste for sheep culture, he should invest in long wool sheep, as they are hardy and easily kept. Sheep however require particular care—more so than any other animal; for whenever the sheep is suffered to grow poor in the winter, very serious loss is manifested in the wool being more brash and less in weight. The true policy to be adopted by all farmers having sheep, few or many, is to have a dry yard or yards for them through all the stormy sleety weather, and sheds constructed with an open space of two feet, if large, and one foot if small at the top and center of the roof, and open at the sides just so as the sheep can pass in and out freely. This will give ventilation, which they must have to be healthy. It is important during the bleak storms which so frequently happen in the winter time, to have feeding troughs running through the middle of these sheds, facing each other, with a center board serving as a back to the troughs; but in strictly dry weather, always feed them in the open air.

Special care should be taken to provide plenty of sweet short grass in summer, with water, and frequently salted, and so on through the winter and spring. During the time which embraces the lambing season, is the most critical, and more importance is attached than at any other period; and the one month while they are bringing forth their lambs, is of more consequence than all the other eleven. For just in proportion as the farmer gives his strict attention to his breeding stock during that time, so will be his profits at the end of the year. I repeat again, that sheep must have good feed and care throughout the year, and instead of losing, as I have seen in the month of March, from sleet, snow and storms, over one hundred lambs and several sheep, all for the want of good warm shelter, this would have been a most profitable increase. Sheep, being exposed to cold sleeting winds, the water freezing on their backs, soon become chilled, great suffering and often death, being the result; and if they do live, the wool, more or less, will drop off. If there is one animal more than another which the farmer should have special feelings for, it is the gentle sheep, when bearing her young in the spring.

For go into that yard which has no shelter, in the morning, after a cold freezing night, and see some of the lambs dead and others which cannot get up, and look at the patient mothers hovering over them and doing all they can to save them, but often to no purpose. Sheep can stand dry weather well, but they are the poorest animal to stand the cold, sleety, freezing rains that often come in February and March. Hence, look out for good shelter, and with proper care and full attention throughout the entire year, no one can doubt that these twenty-eight millions of sheep would produce in wool and flesh, one dollar per head more—an item worth looking at by every farmer.

I am in favor of having corn and oats, or rye half each mashed up by the crusher, and given daily a half pint to the stock sheep each, and the wethers, and the ewes not bearing, should be put in pens by themselves, and full fed for spring sales when meats are most wanted, between hay and grass.

Put into the bottom of your feeding boxes some pure tar in the winter season, and let your sheep eat their food from the same box,; the carbonic gas arising from the tar will keep them free from disease. Feed them now and then, with oats in the bundles, cut up with a straw cutter. This is healthy food and as cheap as any to feed breeding sheep, and three times per week they should have turnips, Mangel-Wurzel are the best; cut them in fine pieces.

The ewes should have assigned them before their time of lambing, a yard, with all the comforts their special situation demands, with a small yard for a nursery to take care of the sickly and fractious if there should be any; I remember well when a boy, of suckling the lambs to their mother; when their bag cake bathe them well, and they hardly ever fail to do well, one of the boys or men should have this duty to perform, and with his patient care much loss will be saved.

These cares and special duties to nurse the young of all your breeding animals is the true secret to the primary success of stock raising, and the farmers who appreciate and realize these facts, the heavier his pockets will weigh with *green backs*, say nothing about the gold that create so many foolish excitements.

It is well known that the rebellion has given an impetus to the sheep growing business; but notwithstanding this, there is no surplus on hand, and with the rapid increase of population, both domestic and foreign, we have no fears of an over stock. But the most important points to look at now, are the kinds and qualities which are best to raise, especially at the present time, from the nature of the facts as they now exist in our own country and England with regard to the demand for long wools. I would advise those who have not a full supply of sheep, to purchase the Cotswold and Leicester sheep; and I think it would be well to make a cross with the Southdown and Merino by the Cotswold and Leicester, thereby producing a substance of wool for the great material wear of our country. My impression is that the warps will continue to be made from our long wools for the present, and for several years, largely so.

I notice from the premium list of the State of Illinois, that Messrs. Brown & Reynolds, of Bates, Sangamon Co., Illinois, has fine specimens of first-class sheep that can be obtained for breeders. Also Samuel P. Boardman, of Lincoln, Logan Co., has a very choice lot of breeding sheep, and their quality would do well to improve on. And I also notice that Mr. I. Grant, of Davenport, Iowa, has some Cotswold bucks that the farmers would do well to purchase for crossing with other grades.

It would be well if persons having the Cotswold and Leicester in the Western States and desire to sell them, to make known the facts through the papers, and I have no doubt they would find ready sale; I also see from the premium list that Canada West was largely represented with Cotswold and Leicester sheep, having breeding qualities, they quite extensively raise those breeds, and they are reaping large rewards from the fact that eastern manufacturers want that kind for their fabrics.

I should think farmers having the means, and are in the sheep growing business, would do well to take the breeders of these long wool, and furnish the demands that are so much needed, and to any person who has a taste and a liking for sheep raising would make a good profitable investment by purchasing largely of these Cotswold and other long wool sheep, having the most available qualities for the imitation of Alpaca and other goods that manufacturers have such heavy demands for, and from the best information I can obtain from my friends in the east, will still continue.

With these remarks on sheep culture, I will close by saying to those who have not taken special pains with their sheep, if they will but follow out the instructions I have given, in my common way, I feel assured they will be benefited by so doing, and to those who are taken the proper care that is needed, I can only say go onward, and you must enrich yourself, and help to strengthen the cords that hold the frame work of our country's ship of State, that is now being put into commission for a long and successful voyage.

CHAPTER XI.

OAT CULTURE.

This product is cultivated mostly for horse food, but the large amount of straw that it bears per acre, and the light draft it makes upon the soil in proportion to the large quantity of food, in all its material forms, it can furnish back to the soil, would seem to warrant a larger culture in the western states.

In the twenty-one states in 1864, there were one hundred and twenty-six millions of bushels arised. Pennsylvania produced the largest quantity—thirty-seven millions; New York next—thirty-five millions; and Illinois next, twenty-five millions.

Now the rebellion is over, I tnink there will be some increased demand in the Southern States, which should stimulate the' farmers of the West to sow more in future. The greatest danger in the cultivation of oats is their tendency to fall down from heavy winds, the straw being tender, when they are full in the milk.

The best soil for oats is a dry rich soil, in order to raise a large crop. You can get a fair crop on poorer soil; but if you have a dry soil of a limey nature, you can have it quite rich, and have no danger of their growing too rank, if you will sow four bushels of seed per acre. This full seeding will take up the rich soil, and being so thick, they will ripen up sooner than if sowed with less seed.

The barley oat is the best seed, being heavy. The black oat mixed with the white do well, as they are stronger; I would recommend half black and half white. I would plough my ground deep for oats, harrow them in well. The low ground on my farm I would put into timothy, so as not to have any wet land to cultivate for grain. How many acres do you think there are in the West of these wet low runs that are under cultivation, and which the farmers plow up every spring in their wet condition, with water and mud up to the horses' knees, and then sown and planted for a rich crop of weeds; but if the grain comes up, it falls down, if oats, and if wheat, it either falls down or is ruined by the rust.

Oats are generally sown on top of the soil, and if rich, will do very well, but much of the vegetable matter lying on the soil will perish, and thus millions of acres of strong rich land is suffered, to my certain knowledge for thirty years in the west, to be cultivated with grain, and lost after so much unpleasant labor in plowing, planting and sowing, and trying to harvest some little grain with many weeds.

I have no doubt but there is in the nine western states, that I located my subject upon, one millions of acres of such rich moist land, trifled with in the manner I have described, which if you put into grass would produce two millions of tons of rich hay at ten dollars per ton, would be twenty millions of dollars more to the farmers, say nothing about all that miserable labor of running your reaper, trying to cut some of the poor grain, and at times breaking your machines by so-doing, and the filthy luck you farmers are always under.

Friends, look at this in its true light, and I think you will come to the conclusion that all such places you have on your farm, you will put them down to meadow, and then you will have clear work before you, and your farms will put on a new dress, changing the aspect of the whole farm, freed from patches, so fruitful to seed your farm with weeds. But now you have it in grass, and when the soil is hard in the winter your cattle will delight to feed on the grasses that will grow so strong.

These remarks emanate from my own practical experience and observations throughout the west, and in conclusion let me say to you, make up your minds at once and leave these pieces out when you plow in the spring, and when the ground becomes dry enough in June, take your team and plow them up well, and in September harrow them well, then sow your seed thick, the ground will bear much seed, and when I pass your farm I shall be well pleased to call and see you, and your improved farming, by cultivating your rich heavy lands into grasses.

P. S. I should remark peradventure, if your oats fall down so that you cannot harvest them all, you have your moveable fences, and you can turn your hogs on them, and they will prudently save them all, and yourself from any loss—the true secret of wise farming.

CHAPTER XII.

HORSES.

Volumes have been written, and can be written on the great available qualities, and rich benefits derived from the various labors of the horse, and no country in the world for the same time has more cause to revere the patient labors in all places required of this animal than America.

From the fact of our wide extended country, when canal nor rail roads were in existence, then it was the horse done the labors of packing and hauling man and his material goods over the country, and who even went in the month of February from Illinois to New York by stage in 1840, making ten miles per day at times through Indiania and Ohio, must appreciate the fortitude of the horse, say nothing about the great endurance manifested by hauling produce to market over the praries, without roads, thirty years ago in the west at certain times in the year; and I don't think I misplace the sentiment of the farmers, when I say they do hold the noble kind enduring animal under stronger attachments, than any others they have under their subjection.

And hence it becomes necessary that the farmers should take the special matter into their own hands, and every township should have their own available well trained seed horse, having the qualities of size, form, muscle, action and durability, that a cross on your best brood mares would produce a good strain of horses, having weight and strength enough that a pair of them would move along, turning up twelve inches deep of the soil at the rate of one and a half acres per day, this can be done with such a team with a high beam plow, and save the trouble of subsoiling in order for general culture; in all respects the strong heavy horses are preferable and will haul much more produce to market, and the extra labor they will do in one year will more than pay the difference in the cost.

Let the farmers look at this in what light they may, the sooner they adopt the measures, the sooner they will save much labor to themselves and money for their pockets—two important items, and worthy their profound consideration. There is no denying the fact that farmers want good strong solid horses on their farms, so that they can do their work effectually. If you have light horses, change them if possible for larger, with persons who want teams for light work. There cannot be any plausible excuse for working small horses on farms if others can be had; and for this available point, commence at once and cross on large horses. It is the height of pleasure to work behind a good pair of horses, that can do your work well and always keep in good order, so cheering to those who like good fat horses.

The most substantial breeding horses for farmers are those that have stood the tests for all work, and whose stock has a durability of standing hard labor, is the Morgan, of Vermont, of which there are many in the west. Farmers would do well to club together and procure one of these animals to cross their best mares, or some other well known strain that will produce the right kind of horses for farming purposes.

Now that railroads are so handy, farmers don't have so much road labor as they did, when their produce had to be hauled from twenty to forty miles. They have also better means for raising colts. Farmers raising colts should keep their mares on the farm as much as possible, and when they wish to wean their colts, they should have a good lot for them to run in, feeding them with slops of bran and corn meal; this will increase their growth; and they should be constantly supplied with plenty of food until they are ready to have the harness on them. It is wrong to think colts can brush along any how, and live on what they can pick up after the cattle. They should never be in the yards with cattle; they are liable to get hooked in the winter; they want yards in the winter, kept dry and warm. There is no animal that the farmer has, that requires more care, with warm shelter and plenty of good food for the first two years, to develope bone and muscle and get all the size possible, the only way stock of any kind can be raised to pay well. All it wants is for the farmers to practice what they know, and the fruits of their farm, in stock and fine colts and horses, will follow; and their other products, under the same influence, will all conspire to cheer the farmer on to grasp all the better features of husbandry; so his accumulating wealth will place him in that position which all humanity are earnestly seeking and trying for—ease and comfort to enjoy life, as the special rewards of his faithful labors.

The best way to feed horses that labor hard constantly, is with oats and corn ground in equal parts, made moist with water sufficient to give it a pliable substance for eating. In the summer prepare it in the morning for the day—adding a little salt; and once a week put in some powdered resin. Twice a year horses should have their sheath washed out with warm water, soap and lard; this is very essential to those in years, preventing disease and even death. A little alum, powdered, is good to give now and then, keeping their kidneys and water channel clear and regular.

When horses are eating grass in the summer time, they are troubled with bots in some cases. When this happens you will always know by the horse being in pain, and he will bite his sides. The most efficient remedy I have tried, was to make him swallow a warm chicken's inwards, and in an hour after drench him with salts, which will give relief. No doubt many know this and other remedies; but if it meets the eye of any who have not tried such, it will serve their purpose.

Much care is required to see that horses don't drink much. When heated in warm weather, very injurious and at times fatal consequences ensue, from the sudden stoppage of the circulation of the blood and air vessels, and when no passage can be effected, they must die. All it wants is caution from those having horses to take care, and know their business, and faithfully perform it, so as to avoid the evils that often arise from carelessness.

At the agricultural fairs in the prairie states of the west can be seen for exhibition horses, of native growth, from the bloods of the best strained horses of our own as well as foreign countries, and are worthy to stand upon any soil, and elicit praise and emulation from the best judges of good stock. Not only is this the case, but liberal enterprising men have been stimulated, for the like of good horses, to pour out their money without stint, to procure out the strength for all work, and the speed and style for carriage horses. Having the true scientific cast to cross with our best mares—which is going forward to enable the farmers, if they are disposed to lay out little money and take the proper pains, which is absolutely required to improve their own stock on sizes that will in a few years supply the farmers with teams, that will richly reward them in every sense that language can place it. It is a well known fact, and should be on the minds of all farmers, that should breeding in and in be tolerated beyond the second year, it deteriorates the constitutional health, and diminishes the bones and muscles, that with all these points engrafted upon all your stock, without rigid care is taken to have plenty of the best kind of food, and pure water adapted to the wants of the several kinds of animals you are raising, your efforts to grow good stock will be in vain. And in just proportion as you manifest this in your labors, will success, that you seem to be seeking after, attend you. May you sensibly realize my remarks on horse culture, that they shall prove to your lasting advantage.

CHAPTER XIII.

POTATO CULTURE.

The potato plant requires more care in the choice of soil, and management of culture than any other root vegetable grown in our country for family use, and I would rather give up all other root crops than be deprived of the rich mealy potato.

And never was this fact more forcibly demonstrated than it was, I think, in 1851, when the potato crop, in many parts of the United States, was destroyed by what was called the potato rot. I can well recollect the great displeasure that rested upon the families in Central Illinois at that time, and with what reluctance I gave up for a time that rich esculent vegetable; and at times since, the people have suffered more or less from the miserable disease of the potato.

It is time the potato disease should cease in our country, and from all the information I can obtain from the farmers in regard to their culture, and the close observation I have taken as they come to market, with a thorough study of the physical laws of animals and plants in reference to these facts, and the possibility of plants becoming sickly and diseased as well as animals, I have constantly sought to learn the cause and its effect, and, if possible, find a remedy to mitigate the potato disease.

In reference to diseases of plants, and especially the potato, I would respectfully say to the farmers, the sooner they reconcile the facts in their own minds that plants are subject to, and have alimentary sufferings in their natural sphere of existence as well as animals; and, I regret to say, for the want of that true knowledge by the farmers they suffer great loss to themselves, and occasion much disease and death to many vegetable plants, so disastrous to their own interests and the whole human family. Hence, it is your bounden duty to look into the inorganic structure of the soils, that you may be able to discriminate the true organic elements of plants so as to assign the seeds to soils most affiliating in their natural wants and desires, so that by proper care and good management you can furnish your soil with all necessary food in kinds that will bring forward the plants to a full sound harvest.

I learn from the best elements known to man, that the constituent organic elements of the potato contain seventy-five per cent. of its entire weight in water, and the balance consisting largely of starch, with some sugar, albumen and gluten, making up the twenty-five per cent., showing conclusively that this plant should always be cultivated on dry, sandy, loamy soil, that will keep the plants growing in the most solid manner possible, and as near to the light and warmth of the sun as they can possibly be cultivated. And from my own experience, and all the knowledge I have obtained from other sources, that potatoes should be planted on thorough dry mellow soil, plowed twelve inches deep, after being made rich with fresh, horse or cattle manures, spread on the ground thickly and plowed in, and then harrowed well, then take your large scouring shovel plow, and run a deep furrow three and one half feet apart each way, and this will throw the rich earth into a square hill, being raised up, and on the top of this soil plant your potatoes, two pieces with two or three sprouts to each piece in the hill, and as near as six inches apart, and the flesh side down if possible; then take your hoe and cover them over three inches deep, at the same time taking pains to form a good round hill, leaving the top over the potatoes twelve inches, and some dishing to hold little water for the potatoes. By this form of the hill you have it so the warmth of the sun and air can strike on your potatoes, that must facilitate them in growing rapidly—for light and heat, with a reasonable degree of moisture, in and round the roots, with the soil being mellow and rich under the plants, the tubers so very impotant will have plenty of room, and having plenty of food, must make a large harvest.

Hence, I entreat the farmers to make a change in their culture of potatoes as I have represented—of course I only mean those who have not adopted the better way to raise what they want for their own use—and that will be an experiment to test the change you will make in their cultivation, but what you do let it be well done, and you will have the benefits of what will arise from the new mode of culture.

Much care should be taken to secure pure seed from those that are raised in dry soil, and are every way sound, for if they have any signs of being diseased don't plant them—better not raise any.

The best that have come to the Chicago market this season are the Peach Blows, they have grown on dry soil and are sound at this time, (January,) and some of the Neshannocks that were raised on dry soil are sound, and many of the largest Peach Blows are hollow. They must have been grown on moist rich land, which will make the potato large, spongy and rotten at the heart. My advise to farmers who have not dry soil, either on level or high ground not to raise any, you had better buy what you want. Your soil will raise corn, grass and of course stock.

The Shaker Russet is a fine potato, but it is only when they have been cultivated on the right soil, but of these three kinds for a large crop, I would recommend the Peach Blow, knowing the seed had grown on dry soil, and a few of the other kinds, to test their qualities.

Then you want a few of the Early Shaw and the Early York to plant in your garden, when by a little extra labor, as I have suggested in my remarks on garden culture, you can have potatoes in June.

The best time for planting potatoes in the Western States for keeping, is when the moon is full in May, or if you don't want to, (plant them in the moon,) say from the 10th to the last of May, and if you hav them on dry soil they will ripen before the frost can injure them.

If you have them on high ground, I would leave them there as long as you dare from the rains and freezing weather, and when you dig them, put them on your barn floor or under cover, and spread them out and let them have the air; I would however spread a little dry straw over them. By this means you can keep your potatoes cool and dry; keep them this way until you have to put them into your cellar, and through the winter keep them as cool as you can in moderate weather. I know by experience this is the true way to keep potatoes in a most healthy condition, so as to have them sound for spring consumption. In my essay for the effectual propagation and preservation of all kinds of seeds I make mention, the importance of the better culture of the potato, which by its unwise culture has brought disease upon them, which must be eradicated if possible—it is the' farmers whole duty to make an effort.

I have seen a statement to-day, setting forth facts that Mr. A. W. Harrison of Philadelphia, has for several years been propagating the potato plant, and by report has succeeded in bringing out two kinds—one early and one late—which from representation is a very superior potato and should be thoroughly tried. There is no mistake, the only way plants can be kept up in their purity, is by experimental propagation in all the available plants cultivated for food.

I notice the mode of Mr. Harrison's culture on the potato. In part it is different from mine in regard to planting; he recommends planting into the furrow eight inches deep, and at the crossing of these furrows drop the largest potato whole, and cover them up to a level surface, being eight inches, and in the culture keep them level. However strongly I recommend all other plants to be cultivated on that principle, only in the last tending. Plants should in dry soil hold the soil highest at a little distance from the plant, so in dry weather in July and August, they will secure little water from the showers so nourishing at these times.

But to plant a whole potato where a large number of sprouts would spring up at one place, would under my practice bring forth too many vines, and too many small potatoes from having them clustered together, which I cannot conceive to be right. While my experience tells me to plant that large potato at least in two hills if not three, and plant them on a raised surface on dry land, on top the original soil, and covered over by the soil thrown up, making a broad hill to hold the potatoes, and retain moisture enough in the soil by having the hill at the top at least eighteen inches, and some dishing to hold water from the showers, so essential to the plants when setting for potatoes, and when they first show leaves hoe the weeds out, and add little soil if necessary to keep the hill high and full, and when you see them begin to bud give them a thorough hoeing by killing all the weeds, and keep the hill full and dishing, and if you have spread on green manure the previous fall, and plowed it under twelve to fifteen inches, and then in the spring put on some old door yard manure, and cross plow that under and make it

mellow by the harrow, and plant as I have directed, I feel assured you will get a good crop of potatoes.

But as I have said before to farmers, if they have or see any different way which would seem to be better, they can surely find out by planting the same potatoes on the same kind of land, and made the same as to manure, lime and ashes, but different in the ways of planting and tending, and also different in the quantity of seed, and also the different kinds of seed; and it is apparent to all that the farmers will raise some good potatoes by these experiments.

These remarks are made from long practical experience of thirty years, and the best crop I ever raised was after this culture, and when you count the labor on the old plan, it don't take much more time, and the result will satisfy all who want to raise good sound potatoes. Reflect, and look at the old plan of plowing furrows and drilling in the potatoes, and then taking same plow and cover them up as I have seen, ten inches deep, where the heat nor the light of the sun can hardly reach the plant, and often have I seen water standing in the furrow when the ground was level, after the rains, causing the water to stand on the potatoes.

Can any one doubt the fact, but that such culture will more or less produce diseased potatoes, when they have to grow in such a watery element as this, knowing from the fact that the plant in its natural state, grown in good dry soil contains seventy-five per cent. of water; knowing this fact, and planting your seed in soil which from its locality must be more or less wet, and

must as a natural consequence imbibe a large surplus of water, which by the constitution of the potato, will greatly enhance the danger of the entire crop becoming diseased even unto destruction and total loss.

These facts will seem apparent to the farmers when they have given this subject its due weight of reflection, understanding the important truths that the *Almighty* in his all wisdom for the blessings of mankind, has out of earth, air and water, formed from fundamental elementary bodies, known as Carbon, Oxygen, Hydrogen and Nitrogin, called gasses, and by their perfect supreme relations they control and hold under subjection, all animal and vegetable matter, showing that the farmers should lead their minds to comprehend the laws by which the operations of nature in the vegetable kingdom are conducted, acquiring knowledge that will instruct them to distribute their pure seeds in soil that will warrant their successful healthy growth, and with your elaborate efforts made on the true systematical principles of cultivating plants, may you receive your rich reward in more abundant harvests, and higher credit for the laudable exertions you will have manifested in elevating the cause of agriculture, thereby benefiting the entire human family; and may the incentives created in your minds, press you onward to grasp the rich treasures that are stored up in the more perfect ways of practical scientific agriculture.

P. S. I see the Harrison potatoes can be had of Mr. A. H. Hovey of Chicago.

CHAPTER XIV.

MULES.

This is an animal I never owned, and the nearest I ever came to own one, was at a time when a gentleman proffered to sell me a pair he had before his carriage. His solicitations being strong, I consented to take and drive them home, some fifteen miles—and if they suited me, I would take them. It was in warm weather, when hard work which setting in an open carriage, was not what I had bargained for, (but as sure as you live,) I made the hardest most unpleasant labor I ever peformed, in the space of four hours going sixteen miles, and consequently I did not purchase the hybrid animals, and I assure you I never have had any desire to invest, most especially for a carriage team.

Hence it is, I have no practical experience in regard to their culture, other than from observations, which were quite extended two years since when in Washington, looking at the immense number of mule teams, taking stores to Grant's army, and of late years they are being used considerably in the west—and do good service farming; and from what I have seen of them, I know they will do well to harrow the soil after it

has been plowed deep—from the fact that they are light, and their feet are small, and better able to walk through mellow soil.

From their toughness to bear the heat and cold, and carry large loads, I should think it would be well for the farmers to have part of their working teams consist of mules, and of the largest kind, which do much more labor, with a trifling more expense.

For those who are plowing their soil deep, and who intend to, I think it would be advisable to have mules with the harrow to pulverize the soil, and to lay off ground for planting, and do all labor on the soil after broken up.

After having said this much in reference to the utility and economy for the farmers, to raise this singular hybrid animal, I will now give a few remarks from the pen of Mr. J. T. Warden of Springfield, Ohio, viz:

The production of so useful a domestic animal as the mule, would not be considered complete without some allusion be made at the outset, to the origin and parentage of this hybrid, though everybody is supposed to be acquainted with the facts of mule breeding—we yet find a great many who do not—and the precise meaning of the terms employed. A mule, in scientific language, means progeny from a cross between two distinct species, either of animals or of plants, which specie however, must be very nearly related, or they will not intermingle. This progeny is generally unfertile or barren, though there are some exceptions to this observation in the first generation of hybrids.

In the case of the horse mule there appear to be but few instances recorded of fruitful intercourse, and none beyond the first generation, though in the case of plants where perhaps the species were less than the reproductions from the first cross. Indeed, this production of mule hybrids, next to the non-production of any progeny as the results of attempts at crossing distinct animals and plants, has been assumed by naturalists to be conclusive evidence of the existence of distinct species. In the practical language of the farm and of the market, the word mule has come to mean the progeny of the male ass, or jack upon the female horse or mare, while the word hinny is applied to the product of the reverse cross of the stallion upon the jenny or female ass. In these two different hybrids containing a similar admixture of blood, we find most remarkable difference of character, which can not be explained philosophically, but which is often cited as showing the relative impress of dam and sire upon their progeny. In the mule we find the general characteristics, such as the head, tail, ears, voice, feet, and temper are asinine, and the males are two or three times as numerous as the females, while in size the progeny more nearly resembles the dam; but in the progeny of the stallion on the jenny, the quality of the horse preponderates with diminished size, this latter quality appearing to depend upon the female.

There is a common impression that the mare which has once been covered by a jack will never again produce a good horse colt, and that she should be kept for mule breeding exclusively. This would make it appear that the male exerts an influence upon the female that is not confined to her immediate progeny, but is transmitted through her to her future offspring. This principle is admitted as established by some physiologists, and the following incident is often cited as proof of the position: a mare that had been covered by a Quagga or Zebra, and produced a striped mule from that cross, afterward had colts that was begotten by three different stallions, each of these horse foals were striped, and resembled the Quagga in other respects. The same is said to be the result after breeding a mare to the jackass. The authority for the above is not given, but is generally admitted to be correct. Mr. Lydell tells us that it may be laid down as a general rule, admitting of very few exceptions among quadrupeds, that the hybrid progeny is stale, and there seems to be no well authenticated examples of the continuance of the male race beyond one generation.

The mule is every way more hardy than the horse, subject to fewer diseases, more patient, better adapted to traveling on rugged and trackless surfaces, less fastidious as to food, and much less expensive in feeding, more muscular in proportion to its weight, and usually living and working to double the age.

Some of the finest Jacks in this country for a long time were of the Maltese breed, the first of which was sent by LaFayette to General Washington, in the year of 1787. He was called the first Knight of Malta in this country, and was highly valued.

After the death of General Washington eight of these mules were sold for two hundred and five dollars a piece. This shows that they were well appreciated at that early day.

Since the commencement of the rebellion the mule raising has been more extensive on account of vast numbers that were used for transportation of army supplies.

For the production of mules, mares should be selected having large roomy bodies, on short limbs, and if a farmer has a taste for raising these animals, and a good share of patience to use them, they will pay well, and for part of the labor on the farm they will perform better than horses, and I hope to see them more plenty in the West, as an acquisition to the farmers' interests, for producing a greater amount of animal labor for the capital invested, thereby more money is in the hands of the farmers, and all branches of industry are benefited, and our country made richer.

CHAPTER XV.

BARLEY CULTURE.

Where wheat, corn and rye can be successfully cultivated, barley will not be raised for bread, not having the composition so desirable for that purpose; but for stock, with the grain being coarsely ground, and mixed with chopped hay or straw, it makes strong feed for horses and cattle—especially for working stock; and the straw if saved in its pure state, is valuable for feeding out in cold weather to young stock, for its healthy, strong, heating qualities, and if put in ricks when threshed, without being wet, and salt sprinkled upon it while you are ricking it, you will find it nearly as good as hay—better than prairie hay.

The grain is largely sought after for malting, for ales and lager beer, which seemingly has no end for that consumption.

For seeding down grass lands in the spring, no better grain can be found than the barley,—hence, under all its availablities, I would recommend to a reasonable extent its culture; it leaves the soil sweet, and is not severe in taking away the strength of the soil, and a good lay for seeding down clover with fall wheat, which will come in on your rotation culture.

I would put on two bushels of seed per acre, of the pure quality. Dry rich loam soil should be plowed ten inches deep, and well harrowed so that all the seed may be well covered; much care should be given to see that it is harvested when the berry is full and bright, and then it should be ricked up as soon as the straw is dry enough to keep.

Bright barley brings twenty-five to fifty cents per bushel more than that suffered to lay in the field and turn yellow in the berry, and the straw will lose half its value.

As I have said before, harvest time should be set apart and considered of the greatest moment; and all possible labor, other than harvest should be suspended, and plenty of strong help engaged to put up the grain in good time, all safe in stacks or ricks, and no farmer should consider his harvest over until all was put up well secured, as I have recommended.

And then the farmers can unitedly join and make the welkin ring, with joyful songs to welcome harvest home.

CHAPTER XVI.

BEAN CULTURE.

The bean is the richest vegetable cultivated, and one of the leguminous pod bearing plants, and more and better attention should be paid to its culture. The necessity of the navy and sea faring people have for this rich plant, should warrant the farmers to procure the little white navy bean for their seed and plant them, in dry soil, having fair strength, made mellow by the harrow.

If free from weeds, plant them three feet in rows, and two feet apart in the rows, put in three to five beans in a hill, if the ground is dry plant them two inches deep. I planted them in hills, three feet each way, which I think is the best, then you can cultivate them both ways cleaning out all the weeds, and on the whole I think the best way.

I have raised sixty bushels per acre of the navy bean; no plant requires more care about seed than the bean, from the fact poor seed mixed with good will produce ripe and green beans, so you have to harvest them together, consequently you have a poor crop, and you cannot get half price for them, and your labor is lost. Hence the importance of having good seed well tended, and when ripe pull them and leave them on the ground in bunches, let them lay one day, turn them over, if the weather is good thrash them immediately on the barn floor, having six men, and they will flail out three hundred bushels in one day; it will not do to leave them out on the risk of bad weather.

Farmers to make money must comprehend what they are doing, and have plenty of help on these emergent occasions, and they will save much time, trouble and money, so essential to those who cultivate the soil.

I am speaking from experience, and hope all farmers will look to their own interests, and all they may do will turn to their entire success; with this, the farmer cannot do better than to plant a few acres of beans, and such as you know are pure, and you can always get the best price. The best soil is a potato, oat or barley lay; it would be well to spread on some old hog and cattle manure after having plowed your ground, and harrow it in; I advise farmers to give them a trial, I think the result will be satisfactory.

CHAPTER XVII.

PEA CULTURE.

The Pea is also a leguminous plant, full of rich nutritious food for man or beast, containing a full share of all organic and inorganic substances, that makes the product strong, and lasting nourishment to animal life, and will grow well on all rich fairly moist soil. From my own experience, I strongly recommend farmers to sow the small Canada pea with black oats, being the strongest to hold the pea up, for feeding hogs, by turning them into the field when the pea is full in the pod. It would be well to try the experiment of sowing them with seed drill, by division of the alternate drill tube. This plan would insure their strength in the soil by being covered deep, and would furnish extra bracing strength with the plants while growing, so essential to their full value, while being eaten up by the hogs. You can arrange your seeding so as to have them come on at three different times, viz : by the middle of June, July and August. This you can effect by having a piece near your hog pasture, so constructed that by a moveable fence, you can, as soon as your first piece has been eaten up, put them into your next lot, and turn your lot just left under, and sow it with buck wheat and English turnips, giving you two crops. The buck wheat will pay you well for your bees, while in blossom, and the grain mashed up, is excellent for stock.

Farmers that have not fully tried this for hogs, I earnestly desire them to do so, and by so doing, you have the best food for your hogs, and especially for the sows and pigs, which no other plants can afford, and at a very small expense. I have turned my hogs into a small lot of peas, and in one week their old coat would fall off, and new life and thrift would take them along rapidly for their fall fattening.

Peas are cultivated quite extensively in the Northern States and Canada, and no plant in its green state will furnish as delicious food for the time they are in that condition, as the Marrowfat pea, that every farmer should cultivate in his garden. This I have spoken of before.

The most suitable as a standard is the Blue Imperial, $8,00; Early Strawberry, $12,00; Dan O'Rourke, early, $8,00; White Marrowfat, $4,00; Tom Thumb, $15,00.

The last named is a very rich small garden pea, and only grows twelve to fifteen inches high, hence the name and are much sought for. They will stand without bracing up. They are worth sixteen dollars more in New York City. I don't know their yielding qualities.

I strongly recommend the farmers to cultivate quite a large plot of these peas the first year to get the seed, and the next year I would cultivate an acre by experiment in the following manner, first take a lot near your dwelling of good soil, and in the fall spread on four large wagon loads of manure to an acre, plow it under ten inches deep—green manure is the best.

In the spring as soon as the ground is dry, cross plow and harrow it well, and as soon as it will do, plant it with the Northern yellow corn, in rows four feet apart, and in the rows six inches apart. As soon as this corn is up cultivate it with a harrow, to take up all the weeds, then take a double cultivator and guage it two feet apart, this will lay off two rows, one on each side one foot from the corn, and in these rows drill your Marrowfat peas by hand, so as to have them in the row six inches apart; cover them over with a light cultivator, and when up, use the light cultivator, dressing the soil well round the peas and corn. I have grown string beans by the side of corn, and make a good substitute for poles. I see no reason why they will not do well for Marrowfat peas. I recommend this as an experiment, and the farmer can try it in his garden with one short row, and that will show whether it will pay; if so you can raise seed peas that will bring fifteen dollars per bushel, paying extra for your trouble.

It seems strange that the farmers living near large towns, don't plant large quantities of these rich peas so to have them early, they always bring large prices. This certainly would pay the small farmers better than any thing else, for early green food for family use.

The quantity of seed of the small field pea should be, on rich mellow soil, four bushels to the acre; drilling is far the best way to plant them, placing the seed all of a depth, having the roots deep in the soil to stay the plants while growing; they being in rows and connected together, must afford bracing strength to keep them up, so essential to insure a sound ripe harvest.

Friends who are not acquainted with pea culture, try them in small quantities as an experiment. All peas planted in rows, should have stays on both sides, to keep them up when bearing. Small stakes driven into the ground, with strips nailed on them, will answer the purpose.

CHAPTER XVIII.

TIMOTHY CULTURE.

The hay product of the twenty-one Northern States, was second in value to any other, being three hundred and sixty-five millions of dollars. Corn was first, it being valued at five hundred and twenty-seven millions of dollars in 1864.

From these figures, the farmers of our country can see the importance attached to the cultivation of the hay crop, and the best ways and means that should be adopted to increase this amount from the same number of acres, and labor expended in its culture.

My first experience in grass culture was in the State of Maine, where the farmers thought more of their haying time than they do out west of their grain harvest; for hay is their great substantial product. Hence, at that early day, all the men, and even the girls, were required to rake hay, and they performed their labor with a will and good cheer, making the meadows ring with their cheerful songs.

From all I have learned on grass culture, I would say to the farmers of the west, take your level lands for your timothy meadows, so they will hold the manures you put on to them. If you have low lands, drain them well, and you have lasting meadows; but if you have any soil you cannot reclaim for timothy, put on the red top, and in a few years it will make good hay.

How many thousands of acres of land there are in the Western States, at this time, being inclosed by the farmers, now standing idle and full of weeds, and propagating seeds to the adjacent lands, and they never fail to furnish a good supply.

Hence the great importance of having all these waste places laid down to grasses. Situated, as they are, they never will fail to produce a large crop, as they must catch the wastings from the surrounding lands, so that all is saved, and changing the features of the whole farm very effectually.

If you desire to raise a crop of grain, when you seed down your meadows in the spring, sow them with barley, leaving the soil in the best condition, having it well harrowed with a fine tooth harrow, and if dry, I would roll or brush the field over. This will put it in a friable form and condition, so that all the organic strength in the soil, for the tender roots of the young plants, will receive food from this judicious process of pulverizing the soil when planting the seeds.

The great utility of this must seem clear to all farmers—after reflecting, the fact that all lumps from the size of a hen's egg and upwards, lying on the top of the soil after sowing your grain, will more or less take the strength of the soil from the plants, by these lumps being dried by the sun, losing the substance they would have furnished the plants if they had been broken up when the seed was sown.

The seed, like all other plants, should be well screened of all impurities. And right here, let me say to the farmers, from the first piece of timothy you cultivate, just before you harvest it, take an hour's time, and go into the best part, and pick out all the foul seeding weeds you can find, and cradle and save this for your seed, and if you have more than you want, sell the balance to your best friend, that he through his neglect or inability, may have the rich favor of sowing pure seed.

My next request to the farmers who are raising Timothy, is to plow their soil ten inches deep on all qualities of land, and if on these rich prairies where the top soil is porous and deep, plow down fifteen inches with subsoil plow, following after with your common plow. Do this in the fall with your grain stubble, and you have a mixture of soil, full of inorganic elements, such as lime, potash, and other constituents that lie plentifully in the subsoils of our so called rich alluvial prairies, in some of the Western States, and especially central Illinois.

By turning up this sub-soil in the fall, the freezing puts the soil in an active healthy condition, by uniting it with the atmospheric gases, diluted with the plastic soil, having the adhesive qualities so essential to sustain the timothy seed in its state of germination, making this culture of sub-soiling far preferable, than seeding on the top porous soils of the rich prairies of the West.

If you have compost manure to spare, it would be well to give this soil a top dressing in the spring, giving warmth and strength to the plants of timothy and grain you have sown with it.

The usual quantity of seed to the acre is eight to ten quarts, I would put on twelve to fourteen quarts, affording more and a finer quality of hay; if the soil is dry I would roll it insuring the seed to take better root; that will give it a strong growth the first season, so to stand the winter without freezing out, and before closing up the ground in the fall put on your roller, and level the stubble down on the grass plants, aiding them safely through the winter.

Never suffer any stock on your meadows, nor any lands, in soft times. This is the most pernicious habit the farmers are guilty of in all their commissions on agriculture, the reasons are obvious, for in the grain and grass fields it entirely destroys many plants and cripple more, wheat especially; it brings out the chess and much small wheat, and the result is it kills out much, and destroys it from being a good uniform crop, that the farmers ever feel proud to see, for the special claims the pockets have on it.

There is one other strong feature in grass culture I desire to mention, which is much neglected in the West, and may seem of small moment to some farmers at first sight.

It is looking over your meadows in the spring, finding out the bare spots the insects have eaten, or the freezing weather has killed out, take some seed, and manure, old chip manure is the best, sow your seed, put on your manure, and put it in with a hoe or spade if in small patches; but if the seed is badly frozen out sow it over with seed, and harrow it in well.

When you have meadows that seem bound down tight at the roots, when spreading your manure on in the spring, take your fine tooth harrow, and scratch it over well, this will take out the dead diseased plants, and give fresh life and action to the entire field, and you will harvest a full crop.

If you have a clear piece of timothy, that will make full plump seed, you can do well to save it for seed, cutting it with a header if you can get it, and thresh it out at the same time; if you cut it with a cradle you will have to bind it up and shock it the same as grain, and stack or put it in the barn.

The proper time to cut timothy, is when the blossom is dropping and the grain is full and ready to turn, and all the leaves at yet green; if you have large fields to cut commence early so as to finish in good time, having grass cutters to work. Now the farmers have great facilities over the scythe, as the cutter; the reel spreads it evenly over the ground it grew on, and it cures well in one quarter of the time.

Timothy grass contains much nutritious sap which requires thorough curing before putting it in barns or ricks, but all grass cut in the forenoon should be raked up and put in cock the same night, and next morning as soon as the dew is off, shake it out well, and get that in the same afternoon if you have good weather. In all harvesting, either grain or grass, the farmers need, and it is essential to have plenty of ready help at their command, in order to save their harvest in good order, making hundreds and hundreds of dollars in their pockets, say nothing of the pleasure they have over the fact that their grain and hay is safe and well secured, and you can thresh or feed it at your leisure.

In conclusion, let me say these are the rich fruits of your wise management in cultivating your farms, on principles of true economy.

CHAPTER XVIII..

CLOVER CULTURE.

Much care should be taken to plow the soil ten inches deep, and having it well pulverized, and the seed put on with a broad cast machine, or you must take a still time for sowing it by hand; it is requisite to have the seed well covered, so the plants can all come up and take a start at once; if the weather is dry you should roll it, and in the spring following it will do well to roll it again, saving much where the frost has thrown up the roots.

These cares and attentions to your grass, and winter grains, is the true secret to the success of making money in farming on that branch of your labors. I lost a crop of wirter wheat I think I could have saved, if I had in time applied the roller to the ground, that would have pressed the soil down, and closed the roots up, so as to save the germ and tender roots. I strongly recommend the roller on grains and all new grass fields; do this as soon as the soil begins to heave up in early spring.

Much care is required to harvest your clover, saving it from getting wet; the grass cutter will facilitate the curing process, as it is evenly strewn on the same ground, aiding very much to get it dry to stack the second day. All hay that has had the sun on it the day of cutting, should be put into cocks the same night, and the next morning as soon as the dew is off, spread it out with a good sun, it will do to put up immediately.

I think clover and timothy hay should have a table one foot from the ground to rest on, saving much loss, that it would have by laying on the damp soil, that must more or less destroy the goodness of the hay on the bottom. I think economy would prompt the farmer not having barns to hold their grains and hay, to look at the means I have recommended in saving wheat and should be adapted to secure all grains and hay, thereby saving much loss from the way it is generally put up.

Farmers can tell with a few figures how much it will cost to have these necessary wants, and I feel assured that one years benefits will more than pay the cost.

I omitted in my statement on wheat culture, to give the full particulars in the construction of the tubing, for saving grain which I will give here, thus: Take four pieces of joist, two by two inches, and as long as you wish for your ricks, and frame them twelve inches square, being the size of the tubing, and put on bars one and a half inches square, with a quarter of an inch taken off at the ends; put these bars on one foot apart, windows at each end, to keep out the damp air when it rains, and with little care to close up the opposite window when the wind blows; you can have the full force of the air to penetrate through your grain, so it will be impossible to retain any dampness in the ricks.

Complying with these suggestions on the clover culture, for the purposes I have herein expressed and follow it up, and no one can doubt your success and prosperity in your meritorious labors of cultivating the rich soils of the West, from whence all other branches of industry must sensibly feel the effects of our farmers' husbandry.

This plant is classed among the leguminous podded plants, and the farmers should render much credit, for its rich food for stock, in a green or dry condition, and for its strong availabilities of drawing the organic constituent elements to the soil, as rich food for the succeeding crop.

Farmers should have the facts in relation to the essential benefits as a manure substance, impressed upon their minds so firmly, that none who have had lands under cultivation for several years, will be found to work his soil without a clover lay, plowed under in June, when in strong blossom, full grown, for preparing the soil for a wheat crop, winter or spring, or for other kinds of grain, that will render the order of rotation of your different crops.

Who, let me ask, understanding in any sense the first rudiments of farming, but will exclaim with pride and joy, at the advancement made by this universal mode of changing the soil, full of life and vigor, to give it a rapid growth, to insure a full ripe harvest for all they have under cultivation.

Your clover field will give you two good crops of hay, and if your soil has been made rich by manures, you can cut your second crop for the seed, which, if taken good care of, will pay you well, for seed at wholesale is worth nine dollars per bushel of sixty pounds.

CHAPTER XIX.

DAIRY—BUTTER.

The statistics of 1861, represent the entire milk product of the United States for the year of 1860, one hundred and sixty millions of dollars, having the following consumption :

Amount in its raw state,		$90,000,000
do	Manufactured into butter,	65,000,000
do	Manufactured into cheese,	5,000,000
Total,		$160,000,000

This estimate was made when milk was very low, only one and a half cents per quart at the farmers' house. But since that time milk has sold for five cents per quart, which would make the entire product for 1860, five hundred and thirty-three millions of dollars. And I notice from the statistics of 1864, there was exported from New York, fourteen millions of pounds of butter, cost price, thirty-eight to sixty cents per pound. which would, to average the amount, make seven millions of dollars, and fifty millions pounds of cheeses. at the average of twenty cents per pound, making the snug sum of ten millions of dollars from these products I also notice in the reports of 1864, in the Eastern

Middle and Western twenty-one States, five millions of cows; and three millions of this number were in the nine Western States. Allowing those in the Western States to have made their quota of butter and cheese, and sold in New York at the prices above stated, the amount for these States would be two hundred and sixty-six millions; but the Western States are extensively engaged in raising stock, and it is not expected they will produce as much of the dairy products as the Eastern States, having the State of New York at their head, until the dairy men of the West will select their cows and cultivate grasses, and take hold of the business with taste and energy to excel the world in the product of butter and cheese.

By the figures above, we see more than one half the milk of the United States is consumed in its raw state as milk, showing strong and conclusive evidence that we want more cows in the country, and strong and thorough movements made in the west for making butter and cheese in qualities to bear favorably with the dairies of New York

My practical experience in the dairy, and the observations for the past ten years in watching the progress of making butter and cheese in the northern part of Illinois, part of Iowa, Wisconsin and Michigan, warrants the fact that choice butter and cheese can be made in those States I have mentioned above, on all rolling land, where the water is running pure, or can be obtained from wells, and the grasses being sweet on the elevated lands must insure rich milk, and with a true knowledge of the dairy business, with all the appliances at hand necessary to handle the milk so it will give up all the rich elements which it contains must insure success.

With the tried experience I have had, and all the lights that have shown upon me for thirty years, I will tell the farmers of the West, and especially those who have a taste to carry on the dairy business, what I understand to be the duties that are required to be performed, by all who desire to make good butter and cheese in the West.

In the first place, your soil should have a rolling inclination, that your grasses will be sweet, affording pure water by wells, or water running through your pastures. The pure Ocean salt, the Ashton brand is the best, being free from lime and other impurities. Much of the western butter is salted with common salt, which will make the butter have a spongy substance, and the longer it stands, the more certain will it have to be used for soap grease.

Having tried several kinds of fine salt by dissolving it in water, I find the Ashton the most free from lime and other mineral substances, that butter must have to keep well, when six months old. With choice cows, sweet food and pure salt, you have the right materials, and with proper and judicious management with all the appliances necessary for the dairy business, fully carried out, success must be the result.

And here I will give the composition of Butter, made by an analysis by the most scientific chemists of the United States and Europe, showing by illustration in one hundred parts, viz :

Casiene, (Cheese,)	4.48
Butter,	3.13
Sugar,	4.77
Saline matter,	0.60
Water,	87.02
Parts,	100.00

This is taken as an average from the many illustrations made by different chemists, which shows most positively, how important it is to have good cows ; and they should have rich nutritious food to increase the richness of the milk, in order to reduce as much as possible the quantity of water that so largely exists in milk.

I know there are many coming from the Eastern States, in addition to those already here, who understand making butter and cheese. To all such I would say, that if they want do anything in the dairy line, and reside on the open prairie, they should plow round some high rolling prairie in the fall, near their residence. This should be done by the farmers in your neighborhood so they can all have the benefits. Then in the Spring take a piece of this and burn it off early, and so on by times up to the middle of July. This will afford your cows rich blue grass food from the native soil, which by salting your cows often will make good butter.

In the absence of tame pasture you should have sown—or better—drilled corn near by, say half an acre to each cow, that you can feed daily, to your milch cows, through the fall, when your prairie grass has failed you. By this management, you can make choice butter through the fall, that will pay you well. By the bye, this corn should be cultivated at all times, to feed dairy cows, making the richest food that can be grown, as it contains more sugar and rich butter substance, shutting out much water from the milk. I think half an acre drilled, on rich land, will supply the cow through the fall, and during the spring months, when most needed, at the time cows are coming in for fresh milking, and the farmers should not fail to raise it, as no other plant has the rich qualities of food for dairy cows. Choice feeding and proper care must ensure good success to all dairymen, while without it, utter failure must be the bitter consequences.

You have noticed that eighty-seven per cent. of milk is water, and the balance is for butter and cheese.

Hence, it must be apparent to all, that to make good butter you must have good pure water for you cows, and without you have your tame pastures, and your cows have to run on the prairies that has no pure lasting running water, you should have a good well at your yard, with troughs enough that your cattle can come to at any time and get water, and if your prairies are fenced up in your neighborhood, the farmers should club together and employ a faithful person to herd the cattle at such places most available for food, and if not handy to running water have wells enough that will furnish all the pure water your cattle want.

I repeat without fear of contradiction, that this is the only way you can make money, and be merciful to your domestic dumb animals, that you know if they could only speak, would storm your ears with words of joy for such blessings rendered them.

In the winter your cows should have room and shelter by themselves at night, so they will not be troubled by the stock cattle hooking them, and their food should be once a day, of oats, barley or rye, ground, and some wheat bran made warm, mixed with this in water, will assist their labors while bearing their young, essential to insure good results, this with plenty of good hay and some roots. The Sugar beet and the Mangold turnip should be cut up and given twice a week to your cows during the winter; this will afford the cows a good relish to nurture onward the unborn calf. If you know near the time when these calves will be dropped, it would be well to have the cows shut away to themselves so no harm can reach them, that they may do well. When you first see the calf, you should assertain if it has'nursed, and if not, you should assist it to do so at once, that the bag may not cake, as often the case with young cows, and if it inclines to swell, put wheat bran into hot water with some lard and bathe it thoroughly three times per day, at the same time have the calf help you, this is the most effectual means I ever found to relieve cows from their pains.

I will suggest that farmers cannot expect to establish their dairies on a permanent basis, without tame clover and timothy pastures, so that they may run into the white honey suckle clover. which is the sweetest food for choice butter.

The dairymen will fill their whole duties, only when they have complied with all the available requisitions that are incumbent upon them, and will be carried out by all experienced dairymen, who delight and take pride in their business.

Hence he will have a milk house, for setting his milk ; the best is what he wants, and from experience and observation, after having tried two cemented cellars, under my houses, I found a higher dryer place was needed, and I made a milk room by taking out two and a half feet of earth, and roofing it over, with a door on one end, and a window in the other, with a fine wire screen on the door and window to keep out all insects, with shelves round the sides and through the center to set the pans on; although this was not made perfect, it was much better than my deep cellars, and the cream would come up well, and with thirty cows would fill a firkin in three days, of choice butter, that I sold in St. Louis for twenty-five cent per pound, the same as the best New York dairies.

I would recommend to farmers who are wishing to make the dairy a permanent business, to build a house near their dwelling, with a cellar deep enough to work in, for packing and keeping you butter in good clean order ready for market.

The size of this house should be large enough to meet your future wants. Material should be brick or stone, with cellar six feet, and the room for setting the milk over the cellar, seven feet, with windows in the cellar and milk room, for ventilation, which is all essential to make pure butter. These rooms should be whitewashed with lime, with salt in it, twice a year. Put no paint inside the building.

If you have not the stone or brick, you can build with wood, by filling in round the milk room with blue clay, packed in solid. It will be cool and do very well. Resting places for your milk pans should consist of three narrow slats, so that the air can come under the pans to facilitate the cream in rising; they should have room between so as to allow the air to circulate freely. The pans, tin or earthen, should be a little flaring, and about fifteen inches at the top. I used tin, and think they are preferable to earthen as to cleaning and breakage. All the milking utensils should be kept in the cleanest and most perfect order, so that no taint may exist in and about the milk house, which should have a temperature of fifty to sixty degrees Fahrenheit, ascertained by a thermometer kept in the milk room.

If you desire to make butter through the warm weather, you can do so, by taking proper care with your milk and cream. I adopted the following means, and made it through the hot weather of July and August. First, I dug a well twenty feet deep, put a windlass and rope over it. Every night I would lower the cream down where it would stand at forty five degrees Fahrenheit, and give it a good stirring when I put it there. If this is not the true temperature for cream, make it to suit the climate, that your butter will come in twenty minutes.

My churn was in the form of a barrel, and as large, with four stationary floats, and a door on the side, ten by twelve inches, made to fit well with a clasp to hold it fast; in the morning early I would take the cream up when it was cool, and in proper condition for churning, and in fifteen minutes the boys could churn forty to fifty pounds of butter in good substance, and would take it out and put it on the butter table, and work off the butter milk with a leaver attached to the table in a few minutes. I put in little salt, and put it into the butter tub, send it down into the well, let it hang at 45 degrees Fahrenheit until evening, then take it out on the table and work it over well, and pack it into firkins, and when full, I would put on a quart of sweet brine made out of a little salt petre and dairy salt, with a little white sugar boiled up and strained, and put this brine over the butter, set the firkin away, top up, so the brine can have a chance to saturate down through the butter; by this process the butter will keep well and be sweet the next spring, and it is the most judicious way to pack it. The firkins should be clean, well seasoned heart staves, neat hickory hoops; have your firkins tared in weight, then always ready for sale; keep these firkins of butter in the coolest place in your cellar.

For small packages—sugar-tree timber sawed into boards—and have pails to hold from twenty to fifty pounds, with a cover and bail, would be more safe than crocks; make them flaring, and the butter will readily slip out, and you can return the pails.

Any person conversant with the dairy business, will have his mind agitated many times if he notices the condition in which butter comes to the Chicago market. Here at times you can see it in all kinds of vessels, from the dry goods box to the flour barrel, so on to the smallest packages of wood and earthen, and in every conceivable shape and form, with color from deep yellow to the white and speckled.

Notwithstanding all this, there is much good butter made in the West, and comes to market in good firkins, crocks and pails, and some sent in balls that were good. Great credit is due to those who have taken hold of the dairy business and made such progress. For well do I remember ten years ago, when I moved to Chicago from Central Illinois, in November, I could not find a jar nor firkin of good Western made butter for sale in the market, and the merchants told me they had to get a winter supply from Buffalo; I purchased a firkin from Mr. Follansbee, that come from Jefferson County, New York; I had some farmer friends in the country, and wanted to purchase firkins, and some dairy salt; I wanted the Ashton, and I could not find any good firkins free from sap and seasoned, nor dairy salt, which surprised me much, when I knew that the Fox and Rock River country was well adapted for the dairy business.

But the fact was, the merchants saw the butter come to market in firkins, that the brine had run through the sap staves and turned black, and salted as a general thing with barrel salt, highly charged with lime and totally unfit for butter.

The people as a general thing, thought they could not make good butter in the West, and consequently those that could, would not do so, and send it to this market to be sold the same as common butter. This prejudice has worn off, and the dairies of Rock and Fox Rivers—and I may say Northern Illinois, Wisconsin, and parts of Iowa and Michigan, are making considerable good butter, and quite a large amount of firkin is also shipped to New York.

Now the duties of those making butter in the West, are simple, when once comprehended and understood. If you send your butter to market in lumps, let them be uniform in size, and in an oblong square, weighing from four to six pounds; they will thus be in good shape for packing, can be handled neatly and will sell for good prices. I saw in the market to-day a box of butter from the country, containing lumps and rolls, in twelve different shapes, and three distinct colors,—the yellow, (good,) the white, the gray, and some being spotted—all winter butter. I ascertained that this butter was all made in one neighborhood, having of course the same climate, air, cold and heat, all alike to contend with. The question may consistently be asked why this butter, coming from the same locality, should be so different in quality, color, form and substance, that to sell it upon its merit, the yellow would bring double what the poor soft, white and spotted would in any market. The cause of this extreme difference is apparent to my mind, and I will offer measures, if adopted and carried out, will plainly show that all this butter could have been made very nearly of a uniform yellow color, and about the same in quality, and all put up neatly in one shape, as I have described above.

In accordance with my own experience in the dairy business, and with the true knowledge of the physical and chemical laws of animals and plants, I shall concede the fact that the yellow butter having a good sweet flavor, was from milk taken from cows having plenty of good nutritious food, either with good clover and timothy hay cut in the right time, when the jucies were full in the plants, and the hay was furnished to these cows, which would give it the rich fresh yellow color, and of course the sweet sap would make the sugar which must make good butter. I will add, that undoubtedly these cows were supplied with some meal and bran at the same time, which would warrant choice yellow butter.

But this milk, suitable to make good butter, must in order to do so, have the proper heat and cold at the time it is put into the pans for rising the cream, so it will come up in a few hours—the sooner the better—hence the importance of having a thermometer to test the heat required to make good butter, and the room where you set your milk in the winter, should be kept to effect that object, and by care this can be done without trouble.

This being the condition of those making the yellow butter, I must, I am sorry to say, assign the cause of the white and spotted butter, to the several reasons, which are first: the cows must have had very poor staled unnutritious food, and a poor scanty supply of water, and suffered to stand in the cold wintery blasts that must distort the system, causing chills that will disturb the functions of the animal, through which the milk fluid must pass, and it is apparent to any reflecting mind, who can imagine for a moment the awful situation of the cow, who is daily and nightly exposed to these severe freezing times, with poor food, that has but little warming gases in it to sustain the vital life of the animal, say nothing about furnishing any substance that would warrant good butter. From such unnatural treatment to the most sensitive domestic animal the farmer has in his possession, and with this diseased substance, called cream, that has been obtained from cows thus exposed, it would be impossible to make good butter under the best management, say nothing about putting this milk away in a cold place, where it cannot render up the true elements in a proper condition to make good sound butter. It is possible that cows being supplied with corn full of heating gases might stand the cold storms, and keep the natural flow of milk so as to make good butter, still the quantity the creature must take to support life would leave a small and some disturbed quantity of milk for butter, that would not be good. All it wants, is a realization of these facts as they exist, and the remedy is very simple and easily obtained, for fifty cents cost, will make a good board shelter to cover each of your cows, and all your grown cattle, with half the price for your calves; this will be an investment of four hundred per cent besides the reputation. I know that there is not a farmer in the West, that will give this subject one hours reflection, but will have these shelters made when fall comes, demanding them to be constructed.

Farmers must appreciate my sensitive feelings, expressed on this all important subject, of taking care of domestic animals, from the fact that I too have been a farmer, who I am sorry to say was not free from all these neglects, and reflection will tell you what my feelings are on taking care of all animals, under the control of the farmers of our country.

The cows that furnished the milk to make these different samples of butter, here represented, should have been tended with good food alike, by having good tame hay well cured, and corn cut up and well saved, to feed cows giving milk, and with the same facilities for rising the cream as I have described, and all things nearly so. No one could doubt the fact that the entire box of butter would have sold for good yellow butter, and at full prices, thirty-five cents per pound, and I am sorry to say that such samples are frequently seen in market, and mixed together, that injures the sale of the better qualities.

The best and most prominent marks for a good cow, are short full head, large mild eyes, rather small neck, deep breast, large body, broad loins, wide hips, full spread bag and teats projecting well to the front, with fine hair and a yellow skin, and color to suit the taste. With such cows, you must certainly have the pleasure of sending to market some splendid butter; I say this from what I know, and feel assured you will have the same results if you adhere to these instructions; if you should fail in one of them, so particular is the management in detail in making good butter, that you may not be able to meet your expectations at first, but don't give it up, try again and you will surely succeed, and in five years there will be a greater change than there has been in the last ten, for the farmers will have tame pastures and meadows more plenty, that will enhance the assurance of choice butter, being made in the Western States in large quantities and rich in quality, put up neatly in choice firkins, having the pure dairy salt, and no person can tell the difference from the choice butter of New York. Thereby setting aside the once conceded opinions, impressions and prejudices that good butter could not be made in the West. And in a few years we will say to New York, the mother of States, for making choice butter and cheese, that you have well instructed your daughters of the West in the dairy business.

But now you are getting advanced in years, while we are young and full of life and vigor, having all the knowledge you can impart to us; we have concluded to make some higher scientific experiments that will test the superior advantages of making butter from milk as taken from the cows, and when it should be fully tested by our best chemists, to ascertain the true temperature the milk should have, in order to produce a more reliable quantity and quality of butter directly from milk, creating an entire economical change in part of the dairy business; the temperature must be increased from fifty to sixty-five when made from milk, and dairymen would do well to give this a fair trial by making some butter from the same quality and quantity of milk, pack it in the same vessels to see the results, and these experiments, being made by those who have the taste and in the dairy business, extensive enough to give a full test, thereby rendering evidences that may prove immense benefits to our country.

Atmospheric churns will be the most available for making butter directly from milk.

Milk, however it may be used, whether fresh from the cow for consumption, or made into butter and cheese, is a product of vast importance, for the luxury it affords to the human family, and the revenue it gives to our country, should stimulate those having a taste for the dairy business, to unite by township, and procure the best breeds of the male and female from wherever they can be obtained, so as to cross with the best stock of cows among the famers. And by this thorough propagation, would begin a new era in the dairy business of the West. Having their best tame pastures of the richest kind, with these improved cast of dairy cows, increasing the qualities and quantities of butter and cheese per cow, so much that our Eastern dairymen, and even England, and other dairy sections of Europe, will have just cause to be jealous of the exalted progress Western dairymen are making, to scale the highest round that can be placed on the standard frame for good butter and cheese. Now in reference to procuring the best stock for dairy purposes, I would say that I copy the following from the extensive reports made by Charles L. Flint, Secretary of Agriculture, to the Massachusetts Stock Growers, in regard to the best breeds of cows for dairy use.

The description of these breeds of cattle are thus given for dairy purposes: The Jersey, the Ayrshires and the North Holland, and formerly known as the Teeswater of which an importation of a bull and four cows was made in 1861, constitutes the herd owned by Winthrop Cheney of Belmont, Mass.

The Holstein cow Texelaar, gave in seven days, from May 27th to June 2d, 1865, seventy-three pounds of milk per day. Her calf, dropped May 15th, weighed at the birth, one hundred and one pounds, which shows the superior qualities for dairy purposes, and good size of stock, as her calf, Van Tromp, bull two years old, weighs 1,700 pounds, and her heifer calf Opperdoes 3d, ten months old, weighs 725 pounds, and the analysis of the milk, made from the four cows, by Prof. Hayes, shows by the statement, that their milk possesses nutritive power, and fattening properties to an extraordinary degree, which would fully warrant the dairymen of the west to procure a male for crossing with the best cows, and in a few years, an increase with other breeds would tell well on the butter and cheese product. Now comes the Ayrshires and Jerseys. They have a fine record, showing that nine and one half quarts of Ayrshire milk makes one pound of butter, which is very rich. The Jerseys are larger milkers, but the milk is not so rich. From the prices of these cows and their calves, as I learn from a sale of Jersey cows and calves, made at the farm of John Giles, of Conn., that Jersey cows brought $293, on an average, and calves an average of $85 per head, and the heifer calves will sell for $50, as soon as they are dropped. The Ayrshires will sell for nearly as much. These are reliable facts, and would seem to arouse the farmers up to a sense of their true interests, and especially those who desire to carry on the dairy business in the West, as one branch of their cultivating the soil, which, if properly attended to, will give you rich results for your worthy labors so nobly rendered.

CHAPTER XIX.

DAIRY—CHEESE.

When we contemplate the amount of money that is invested, and the large quantity of produce obtained from this source of husbandry for home consumption and exportation, it is well to inquire of the dairymen, whether the results of their labors in the manufacture of cheese are satisfactory.

When we look at the different qualities of cheese in market, and the variations of prices, we wonder why it is these prices vary so much, and the only answer we can give is in the manufacture, as the milk taken from the cows is much the same, and should produce the same kind of cheese, if the same management had been applied to it.

My experience in making cheese is light compared with butter, but from the observations I have made in the State of New York, warrants me to say that all the utensils used in the cheese room should be well cleaned, and the dairy room sweet and well ventilated.

The milk is taken to the cheese room and strained through cloths, so as to take all extraneous matter out, and take a little annotto, dissolved in a little water, and strain it with the milk, only to give the curd a rich cream color; the rennet is of much importance, for unless this is pure and sweet it is impossible to have good flavored cheese.

When the milk at the expiration of thirty minutes is sufficiently coagulated, which experience alone can determine, a thin wooden knife is used to cut through the curd to the bottom of the tub each way, leaving it in squares, then let it stand until the curd settles, and the whey will be upon the top, then dip this off in a cloth placed in drainers, leaving the curd in the tub nearly dry.

Now comes the process of cutting the curd with a cheese knife, to facilitate the whey to run off, subjecting the curd in the mean time to a light pressure. In a short time, cut it in quite large pieces, and placing it in a tub covered over, letting it remain until the next morning. Then take this, with the curd from the milk of the previous evening, cut it into small squares with curd cutter or knife, pour warm water over it, stirring it well, adding water still warm, till the curd will yield to pressure without breaking; then dip it into drainers, and stir it until nearly cold and free from moisture. It then must be salted with good pure dairy salt, about two and a half pounds to one hundred pounds of curd. When the salt is added, it should be thoroughly stirred, that it may all be well incorporated, and when it is cooled sufficiently, lay a cloth in the hoop, and then your curd, and press it down with your hands as it is put in, to make it as solid as possible. If you have more than enough for one cheese, you had better divide and put it into two hoops, with uniformity of size.

It is then put to press, and pressed gently at first, increasing the pressure at times for an hour or two, till sufficiently firm to take out and turn again, changing the cloth and letting it remain forty-eight hours. Be sure to take it out once during the time and turn it. After this, it is ready to be removed to the dairy room, and dressed with oil made from the whey butter. Then add a little more annotto, if you like the color, and place it upon the shelf. The cheeses are all turned daily, and dressed with the oil of butter.

Much care is required in handling your cheese when turning and rubbing them, as at that time they are tender. The cheese room should be at about fifty to sixty degrees Fahrenheit, kept free from all insects, with fine netting screens, having windows and doors to let in the air.

The curing and taking proper care of the rennet is of great importance, being the stomach of the calf, and from those that are fat, the rennet is the best. When the calf is killed, it is taken out, the contents partially emptied, then placed in a deep dish to remain twenty-four hours. It is then stripped through the hands, and put on to a plate, and covered over thickly with pure salt, to remain thirty hours; then turn and stretch it over a bow, rubbing all the salt you can upon it, and putting all you can inside. When it is well dried, the bow is taken off, and it is put into a linen bag and laid away where nothing can touch it. When it is required for use, put one skin into two quarts of warm water, rubbing it occasionally. After soaking twenty-four hours, remove it, and add two quarts of strong brine to the liquor; strain the whole into a vessel that can be covered tight, and keep it in a cool place, adding salt occasionlly, so there will always be undissolved salt at the bottom. Having it prepared in this way, it will keep sweet and always be ready for use, requiring only half a pint to curdle forty gallons of milk in as many minutes.

You can ascertain the strength of the rennet by trial, and use it as required. Rennets improve by age, and should never be used until one year old if you can possibly help it.

There is no mistake about it, the dairy business for making butter and cheese will rapidly increase in the west, wherever the soil and water is best adapted for it, and there are many dairymen in the west making butter and cheese; already there are several cheese factories started, and more, I learn, will start next season.

In this manner of making cheese of the milk from the surrounding farmers, it saves the women some labor, but, I think, by using up the milk in this way, it must enhance the value of butter, and I would advise those who have the means and a taste for making butter, having good pure water and grass, to make butter, as it must bring a good price. I think the dairymen will see it in that light and improve the opportunity, I mean those who can make good butter, and there is no doubt of the result as to prices. I do not see any reason why there should not be butter factories as well as cheese factories, and those who thoroughly understand making butter, and having all the means and appliances at hand to purchase the milk from the farmers in the surrounding neighborhood at a fair price, so as to make money to pay for their worthy labor. This plan looks feasible, and with a spring carriage having two vessels big enough to hold what milk you could get up, you could divide the qualities. Under this management, it places all the milk into the hands of one who is capable, and can afford to supply himself with a milk-house, and have all things done by the most scientific rules, for the assurance of making choice butter.

I truly hope a number of factories will start in Michigan, Northern Illinois, Wisconsin, and in the eastern half of Iowa.

All that is wanted, is for those who know how it is done to procure the best heart-seasoned firkins, made neatly, with smooth, trim hickory hoops, and have for ready sale, some neat boxes made from sugar tree boards, an inch thick, flaring so as to let the butter out easily—to have a cover shut over with a moulding round the top, and a little neat padlock to make them secure to come to market. The boxes can be in sizes to nest up, which would facilitate returning them back to the country—saving much trouble and loss in breaking jars, that often break in carrying to market.

These boxes can be tastefully made, and obtained at Chicago cheaply, as they can be made by machinery.

When dairymen or merchants want to send butter to market in warm weather, they should have ice, or when the grass is sufficiently large, should cut some early in the morning, and pack round their butter in the wagon or cars, and it will be in good order when opened. This will keep the life and substance of the butter unimpared, which is of the utmost importance, to have it sell for good prices. From all the practical experience I have had in making butter, I think this can be carried out profitably by those who will engage in the manufacture of butter and cheese as I have recommended.

All branches of people in other pursuits of life, who can depend upon those making butter and cheese, will feel grateful to those who have taken hold of the enterprise to furnish a more constant supply of these great luxuries so essential to good living. My highest wishes are that the dairy business will be carried forward to meet the wants of all, returning rich rewards to those who devote their time and money in such an important business.

I learn that butter factories are successful in New York.

CHAPTER XX.

BUCKWHEAT CULTURE.

This plant will grow well, and is quite extensively cultivated, the product in Pennsylvania in 1865, being five millions of bushels, in New York five millions of bushels, and in Ohio one million of bushels. It will do well on all dry, sandy, rich, loamy soil, but will do very well on poorer soil. Having a light draft on the strength of soils, and a choice exterminator of weeds, killing all such noxious things that the lands may be infested with, even the common thistle.

From my experience and observations I am fully satisfied that the rich prairie soils of the West, especially those that contain a deep rich moisture, produce flour that is black, and not having that rich pleasant flavor which is produced in lighter sandy soil.

Hence I advise all having such land, not to cultivate buckwheat. The best lands in the West, as a general thing, are the light pine lands of Wisconsin, and I would recommend her farmers to cultivate double what they do, at any rate on their poorest lands, which, with a little manuring, will produce from twenty to thirty bushels per acre.

On poor, sandy light soil, it would do well to sow buckwheat, and when it is full in the blossom, plow it under as a fertilizer, and let it rest over until next year. Then in June plow it up, and at the right time sow it with buckwheat again, making a very good crop.

During the winter the flour has an extensive sale in all the States, and in those States best adapted to its successful growth as to quality and quantity, the farmers will do well to take their poor sandy soils and make a business of it, procuring choice seeds, grown on the right soil, so that the inhabitants of the country may know what buckwheat cakes they want, by paying a fair price for them, that those raising the choice wheat and ready to sell at a fair price, may have a chance to exchange. As far as the buckwheat is concerned, if my land was not full of sand I would not raise it.

CHAPTER XXI.

POULTRY—CHICKENS.

Domestic fowls have been raised and eaten as food since the early days of the history of the world, and are still held throughout all countries as a luxury for food, but to have it sustain that estimation, it must be well tended, with proper food, and have comfortable resting places, summer and winter. From my own experience, the farmers of the west do not put the true value and estimation on poultry, and hardly any attention, in any respect, is given them. This is wrong—for if the farmers allow the poultry to live on their farms, economy and justice should require them to have plenty of food at all seasons of the year, especially in the winter. In this light of the subject I will give my views on feeding, shelter, and all that pertains to the better care of the poultry yard.

The first thing, the farmer should make up his mind how many hens, turkeys, geese and ducks he may want, and if there is a selection to be made, to take what he wants for his own family through the year; but as he has to make provision for that many, he can just as well give little more room, then he can raise three times as many, and by feeding them well and having them fat, he can always get a good price for them, especially early in the fall and late in winter. With proper treatment, hens will lay all winter, and the eggs will always sell at high prices.

After having made up your mind how many hens and turkeys you will keep, which are the most sought for, and of course the most valuable to raise. I will take as a basis, one hundred hens, and you want a shed thirty feet long and twelve feet wide, with ten feet assigned for their sleeping room, which must seem better than if they were on the fences, in the trees, or, for choice, some of them are in the horse stable, resting on the stalls or on the horses in very cold weather.

Reflection will tell you, this does not pay to have your poultry take their chances to live through the winter, having many of them die from exposure. The best timber for making resting poles are sassafras, fir and spruce, resting on ledges, so that they can be taken often and washed with strong soap, to keep off all insects. The best plan to put these poles up is to commence on one side and put the first pole two feet from the ground, and raise the next pole four inches, and so on with each until you have them all up, so that each tier of birds will be raised so as to afford better ventilation than if they were all on a level. The ground should be made hard, and two inches of sand should be kept on it at all times, which will serve well for the poultry to eat what gravel they may want, and it can be readily raked so as to take all the manure off—do this once a week, and have windows, which will serve to give free ventilation. These windows should be on one side near the bottom, and on the other side near the top, so as to give good ventilation, the wind would not then strike directly upon the poultry; it would be well to have these windows long and narrow, with wire screen to keep out all insects. The windows on the lower part will serve to admit the hens in and out. The next twenty feet should have a floor five feet from the ground, the basement of this room, being supplied with troughs, will do well to feed your hens in, and over this room should be the nursery—laying in one half and setting in the other; between these two rooms, have an open partition affording ventilation. Let this floor be raised from the center to the walls so that they can be washed out frequently to insure health. In the rear, connected with this house, you should have an acre of ground put into—say one quarter to timothy, one half to oats, sown at different times, so as to make the food last longer, and the other quarter put into common tomatos, and buckwheat with millet, all being good food for poultry while green, and when ripe. Have this yard made rich to give a large growth; sow the oats thick, this will give all plenty to eat and a healthy place to bask in the soil when it is dry. When the chickens are old enough to follow their mother, partition off a piece of this yard for those having chickens.

The next thing under consideration is the breeding stock; and the number you want, depends upon how large your family, and whether you desire to raise any chickens or eggs for market. If for your own small family, twelve hens and two male birds will be sufficient; you must see that the latter agree well together.

It requires much care in selecting fowls. Having your stock selected, the next point will be the breeding. I would prefer young birds for this purpose, and would select from the pullets in the Fall, that were well grown, and take two year old male birds for them.

It is well to introduce new pure breeds into the yard in succession every two years, so they cannot degenerate. There is no danger but that hens will do well in hatching, if they are well fed, and have good coops for that purpose; size of coop eighteen by twenty-four inches, closed on all sides except the front; the front can be made of slats placed close enough together to keep out rats. You can have three of these slats put together so as to raise up, to let the hen out for her food twice a day, when setting. Much care should be taken that they have plenty of pure water, and their food regular. Their drinking vessels should also be kept clean. It is a good plan to keep some gravel at the door of the coop, so that they can take what they want. The first week the chickens are hatched, they should have bread crumbs soaked in warm milk or water, and tended carefully. Wheat and corn steamed are good food for hens and chickens. They should have good food three times a day in the spring, and through the summer in proportion to what they have of green food. Much advantage is gained by having your hens set early, this will give you good chickens by middle of June, and if you have any to spare, they will bring a large price. The object of raising poultry is to have some always ready to use as food, they will always be appreciated; when they are tended well, the chickens and capons are good.

In the fall, what male birds you do not want to keep over, you should select them out and put them by themselves, feeding them with coarse ground meal, steamed, and like soft pudding, with pure water. Feed three times per day, early in the morning and late at night; put into their room, every other day, some pulverized charcoal, to keep them in good health, to insure which, their trough should be washed out often. If there is any fighting done to any extent by male or female, they must be separated into a pen, for such fowls, by unsteady feeding and exposure to cold storms, become more or less diseased, and it is hard to get them up again. All that is wanting, to have good fat poultry, full of health and life, is to have a comfortable house, kept clean, plenty of good food given regular and pure water. Clean out their night soil twice a week, and feed them through the winter with some cabbage tops green, a little at a time, and give them sound offal meat, cut fine, with boiled or baked potatoes mixed with meal. Keep lime in their houses constantly, and you will have no trouble in raising chickens, and have them always ready for eating If the farmers don't use proper care in raising choice poultry, they will save money to let them alone; for one-half of the chickens that have come to this market, were medium, and some very poor. Many would spoil for want of sale, and had to be thrown away. This was unfortunate for those raising them, as they could not have paid any profit.

The farmers for themselves, and those living in cities and towns would be better off, and a great blessing would eventuate to those who are able to purchase good poultry, if they could obtain them from the farmers, where all the fruits, vegetables and meats, whether good or bad, must be procured. I truly hope the farmers will see the remarks I have made, and those who like to raise choice poultry will realize in full what I claim on taking good care of domestiic fowls.

POULTRY—TURKEYS.

The impatient wanderıng disposition of the turkeys render them unfit company for other fowls whose habits do not require so much room. Farmers having calf pastures can well raise turkeys, as they will do with a little food for their young during April, May and June, and as soon as you get your grain off your fields, you can let them run there, and they will do exceedingly well in picking up grain and insects, which they relish and greedily devour. By feeding them once a day, you have the assurance of their safe return at night, and they will keep growing finely through the summer and fall ready for an early market for your oldest broods.

Like all other species of animals, care is required to make good selections for your breeders. Both male and female should be full, plump in size, with fine bright plumage, clean legs. The most hardy are the bronze in color, with a lively animated action. The hen breeds when a year old; they are better when two years old, and will do well at three years. I would change the male every year with your neighbor, to keep up strength. From the first to the middle of March, they begin to lay, and show signs of this by a peculiar cry and strutting around with self-importance, searching in quest of a secret place for incubation; she should have a nest made for her, and use gentle means to have her lay in it; the nest should be made of dry straw, and secluded away from being disturbed; it would do well, as an inducement to draw her to the nest, to have a piece of chalk made in the form of an egg, and put into the nest. The turkey hen is a constant setter, and very loath to leave her nest even for food; she should have regular food. After she has finished laying, it will take four weeks for the chickens to leave the eggs, and these, like other young fowls, do not require food for several hours, when they feel inclined to eat, nature directs them how to pick it up; eggs boiled hard and finely mixed with crumbs of bread are good, oat meal with water is good. The turkey hen and chickens, should be housed for a few days:: in fine weather let them out; should a shower come, they must be taken care of and put under shelter. This treatment is required for a few weeks, after which they can take care of themselves. As they become older, they require some meal until the harvest fields are clear, then they can fare as well as the old turkeys. Taking care, and having a pride in them, is the great and important secret of success in rearing domestic poultry. These turkeys furnish much good food any time in fall or winter, and especially in the holidays, and at times they will bring a large price, and a great luxury to town and city people who have not the facilities to raise them; therefore, interest and duty as a favor would seem to invite the farmers to cultivate a goodly number of turkeys.

GEESE AND DUCKS.

Are choice water fowls, and held in high estimation by some people, and should be reared by all who have a taste for such fowl, and especially when they have a small running stream through their pastures, then you will not have much trouble to raise them, being easily kept by grazing, as they are both hardy fowls; but while they are raising their young they should have food similar to other poultry. One gander is enough for five females, and is very attentive, vigilant and daring in their defence. They too will hatch in a month, and when the goslings are young, they are tender and want care and the same food as turkies.

With all the ducks, the Aylesbury are the best, they are white and very quiet, and make a rapid growth—plumage unspotted white—and are the most profitable to raise; I would advise those who desire to raise geese to raise ducks also, for they require the same nursing and food, and live peaceably together.

THE MODEL FARM.—160 ACRES.

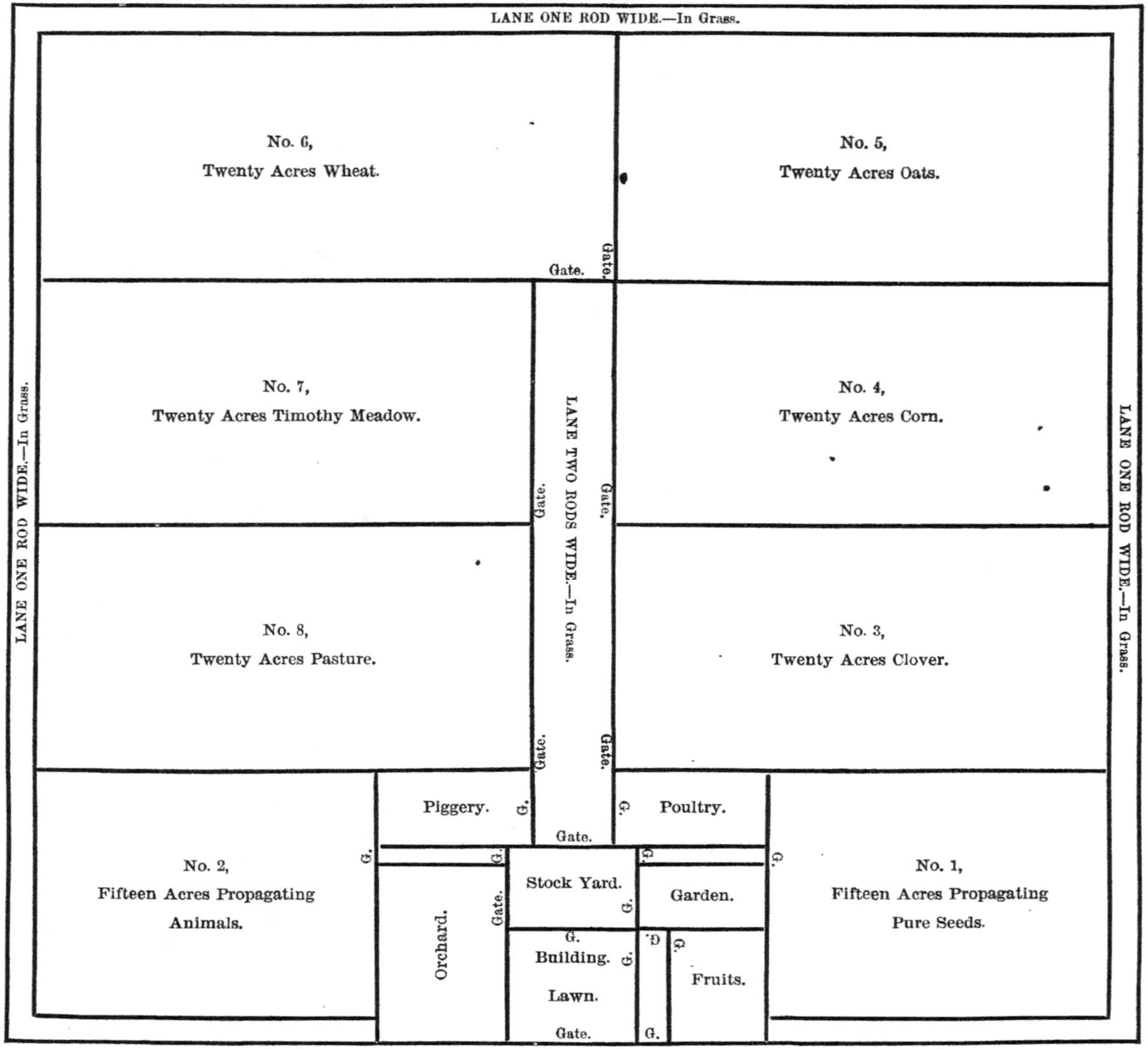

LANE ONE ROD WIDE.—In Grass.

No. 6,
Twenty Acres Wheat.

No. 5,
Twenty Acres Oats.

No. 7,
Twenty Acres Timothy Meadow.

No. 4,
Twenty Acres Corn.

LANE TWO RODS WIDE.—In Grass.

No. 8,
Twenty Acres Pasture.

No. 3,
Twenty Acres Clover.

Gate. Gate. Gate. Gate. Gate. Gate.

No. 2,
Fifteen Acres Propagating
Animals.

Piggery. G.

Poultry. G.

Gate.

Orchard. Gate. G.

Stock Yard. G.

Garden. G.

Building. G. G.

Lawn.

Gate.

Fruits. G. G. G.

No. 1,
Fifteen Acres Propagating
Pure Seeds.

LANE ONE ROD WIDE.—In Grass.

LANE ONE ROD WIDE.—In Grass.

CHAPTER XXII.

MODEL FARM.

I have made a diagram of one hundred and sixty acres of land designed for cultivation, and from experience and observations I have had on agriculture, I am persuaded that all farmers as fast as they are able, should make these improvements near as circumstances will permit. I have assigned five acres for the homestead which should have the fruits and garden as I have recommended in another place, and the two fields of fifteen acres should be devoted to the propagation of animals and vegetables, and one twenty acres gently rolling should be selected for the durable pasture, and one, the most level on the farm, should be taken for the lasting timothy meadow, situated so it will receive the washings from the other fields, so essential to furnish the organic food to give it a large growth, and the balance four fields of twenty acres each, are assigned to raise the cereal products. The most effectual way of cultivating the soil, is by rotation of crops, having two objects in view, to rest the soil by following a crop with another, which largely subsists on different elements, increasing its carbonaceous matter by such crops as will add much to it in rotation, having both these special objects in view.

It is true, the longer the soil has been cultivated, the more necessity of a clover lay, and rotation crop culture so essential to supply the soil with organic food to insure a full harvest. I have left lanes round the fields one rod wide, for passing to and from all parts of the farm, where labor is required to be done. When these lanes are all put down to grass, as they should be, in good order, they will essentially afford a double benefit, by stopping all the weeds that generally grow round the fences and turn-rows of the farm, which keep them well seeded with noxious weeds, whereas now they will raise a good crop of hay, at least five tons, and greatly improve the looks of the farm. With all the low places cultivated in grass, there will not be one rod of waste land on the farm. To make the farm complete for water, there should be four wells on it, one at the house, one at the cattle yard, in connection with your hog and calf pastures, and one at each junction of your middle center fields, as described in the model. The center lane should be two rods wide for turning purposes; these wells should have conducting spouts to supply stock in four of the adjoining fields, when needed; gutta percha is the best and most economical in the end.

These two fields, number two and three, containing fifteen acres each, should have for commencement a summer fallow or clover lay, and what is designed for fall wheat, should have a cross plowing twelve inches deep, well pulverized with a harrow and well drilled in, and in the spring cross-plow the balance, and on all, except where the small grains are to be sown, haul on two cords of old manure to the acre; do this in the winter, and leave it in piles, and spread it over after cross-plowing in the spring, and have it well incorporated with the soil by the harrow.

Before sowing any grain, measure off the tracts assigned for each product, and between your different grains plant beans, peas and potatoes, so they cannot intermix.

I have given below what in my judgment would seem best to cultivate and carry out by experimental culture in different ways, so to test the most available way that all plants should be cultivated, and thereby obtaining the largest profits from the soil under all the labor and money expended. I here annex in detail a list for cultivation, viz: one acre of pure White Corn; one acre of pure Yellow Corn; one acre of pure Mixed, to hybridize; one acre of pure White Winter Wheat; one acre of pure Red Winter Wheat; one acre of pure Rio Grande Spring; one acre of pure Iowa Amber Spring; one acre of pure of all grades of Winter Wheat; one half acre best Rye Winter; one half acre best Rye Spring; one half acre best Barley Oats; one half acre of all grades of mixed Spring Wheat; one acre of four of the best grades of potatoes, with my advice to cultivate the most of them as I have directed in my essay on potato culture. There are one and a half acres left to experiment with any plants you may desire.

The true intent and object of these experimental propagating grounds are to bring out, by superior culture, the strong vigorous growth of the several plants which the farmers generally cultivate, and when harvest comes, take a basket and go to the field, and with special care, cut the most ripe, large, prominent heads of wheat—keeping each kind and name to itself, and lay them in your lofts to cure; when well seasoned, take each head and shell off some at each end, then shell the middle and put them carefully away; you should try to obtain enough from your first crop to sow an acre of the different kinds of spring and winter wheats—that is, if your soil will produce both kinds successfully, and so on with your different grades of grain. Take your bag and pass through your corn as soon as the husks begin to open, and those ears that hang down, weeping for their heavy weight, with their clothing loose and ready to take off; from these careful selections you can procure seed enough for your own use, and perhaps have some to sell to those who do not think it necessary to prepare grounds for propagating pure seed; true, there may be many who are not prepared to make these improvements—to such, you can well supply; so you will go through the balance, and procure the well-developed ripe grains that exhibit a vigorous growth, treating them in the same way, and having them well secured in medium warm places, where severe freezing cannot come to kill the germ, and none will doubt the rich results that must spring from such a worthy enterprise.

Remember that kind begets kind, and for your wise labors, you have the assurance that these sayings will prove true by your laudable efforts.

Field number three is designed for pasture and feeding grounds for cultivation and improvement of the better grades of domestic animals, so essential to the highest interests of the farmers, and extending untold benefits to all branches of industry. Hence, all farmers that are able to have these fields set apart for the special purposes of procuring pure and better seeds the sooner they resolve to take hold of this noble life-sustaining enterprise, will their names be inscribed as benefactors to our country's greater good.

In the economy of nature, and by the fundamental laws underlying all forms of life, animal as well as vegetable, that in order to insure the finest issues, the two should go hand in hand, and whatever the farmer does for one, interest impels him to do for the other. Hence, we see at a glance, the imperative obligations resting upon all that are able to make these propagating improvements as fast as time will permit; what occupation of life can a man more fully gratify his feelings, than to cultivate the plant and rear the animal under scientific principles.

With these fifteen acres devoted to stock culture, under a high state of cultivation, to supply nutritious grasses for the support of a few choice stock breeders in cattle, horses, sheep and hogs, to be used for the propagation of the best grades of these four different leading animals of our country, by a judicious crossing with the best native breeds, must arise new features in the minds of those who cultivate the soil.

I will put the question to the farmers of the West, to this effect, viz: Suppose that five farmers of each township throughout the country, should adopt this special mode of improving their seeds in vegetables, so that by the right culture they can raise one hundred bushels of corn per acre, fifty bushels of wheat, seventy-five bushels of oats, seventy-five of rye, and five hundred bushels of potatoes, all under the propagation of pure seeds, and planted on the farm by rotation of crops. How long would it take for the balance of the farmers that have a start, to accomplish the same results.

As you are not present to give the answer, I will assume the responsibility to say, that within three years, every farmer in the West, according to his means, will have a show of this improved culture on his own farm, having a clear field before him, stimulated by the influences wrought in their minds, by the increased products of the soil, will produce an entire new aspect upon all the labors of life, and the tillers of the soil will have their physical, intellectual and mental powers brought up to a more perfect state of harmony, that their future labors will be lighter, and their ways more pleasant to perform all the duties of life, showing clearly that Agriculture is one of the noblest works of nature, and no farmers in the world have the advantages to elevate the cause of Agriculture as those in the West.

You will notice in my representation of a model farm, I have placed the homestead in the center, in all respects, if the location is most elevated, this would be the proper place; but where ever the homestead is located, the division of the farm can be made just as advantageous in every respect as though it was in the center.

To make the line of fencing which I have laid out, there would be one thousand rods, which would cost two thousand dollars. On an ordinary farm about five hundred rods would inclose the farm and fence in the homestead with the cattle yard; whereas, the farm I assume to be a model one, has eleven separate fields, beside the cattle yard, at an expense of one thousand dollars in extra fencing, which, at ten per cent interest, would be one hundred dollars, and one good steer, at four years old, would pay the interest on this splendid farm of eleven fields—affording all the advantages of fruit trees, garden, four small and large pastures, one meadow, two fields for propagation of animals and plants, and four fields of twenty acres each for raising the usual products.

Now, friends, who cultivate the soil to make money, let me considerately ask you to give my remarks on the model farm a candid, impartial reflection, as to its merits and demerits, and upon that decision will rest your future action; I am persuaded that when that judgment is finally rendered, it will be on the side of making the improvements as fast as time and means will allow, and those who have the means will perform the labors as soon as possible. For the reflection they have given this subject will convince them of the following facts, which are beyond contradiction, viz:—You have your pastures of tame grass for all your animals according to their several wants; you have your rich meadows for your hay, and affording rich grazing in the fall when your pastures are short, and you have four fields of twenty acres each for raising your grain, which, if cultivated under the rotation system from the clover, wheat, corn, oats and barley—with all these, you have one field of fifteen acres for experimental growing pure seeds, which of itself is enough to pay all interests on extra improvements, and last, though not least, you have fifteen acres set apart for propagating pure breeds of stock, that will render invaluable wealth in crossing on the best common stock, which is the lasting and sure prosperity of all who cultivate the soil.

In conclusion, I desire to say, that the lanes and roadways around and through your farm, which I have taken in the model farm account, should be well put into meadow grass, instead of having them as may be seen through the West, thousands of farms with their fence corners and sides, with turn rows all growing a crop of weeds, which will blow over and seed down your farm that has been cultivated; they never winter-kill, and the farmers have them to choke down and labor hard to destroy.

There is another important feature in this model farm; by having the fields all fenced in, when the elements break across your fields of waving grain, which is nearly ready for harvest, tearing it down so that it cannot be saved, what pleasure there is in the fact that you have these fields well fenced, so that you can turn your stock into them, saving much that would, without this fencing, be lost; then, too, as soon as the grain is taken from the fields, the stock can be turned on to them, where they will eat up the offal and the seed that often rattles out when fully ripe.

So with all these many advantages, growing inevitably out of and from this improved invaluable means of cultivating the soil, must commend itself to the entire masses of the farmers of the West, and arouse them up to bend all their strength to put what means they can spare to make themselves better off in wealth and health, which, together, control the destiny of mankind.

CHAPTER XXIII.

HEDGES FOR FENCES.

Fencing in some form, has been in use ever since the early days of the world's history, by all nations. Thus we find, in the early times of our own country, that laws were made designating what should constitute a sufficient fence to restrain all reasonable domestic animals from committing trespasses. To this end the farmers of our country have labored long and much to build and sustain their fences, to satisfy the laws under which they were living, and no part of the United States, at the time of its settlement, was so destitute of timber as some of the Western prairie States ; of these States, there has been much of the timber taken for building and fencing, and the balance must of course come high ; the farmers have to fence much of their old and new lands with pine lumber, and the large demand for building material and fencing will come high in future in consequence of the immense territory it has to supply.

Now, friends, under all these existing circumstances, I desire to say, as one of you, who have made the fences for twenty years in Illinois, understanding that when lumber is twenty dollars at the market places, that it will cost two dollars and twenty-five cents per rod for fencing. Every farmer possessing a farm of one hundred and sixty acres, in order to reap all the benefits of his farm, should have, exclusive of division fences from those adjoining him, one thousand rods, to be complete to save all the profits from the farm. At this stage of the subject, I will re-affirm what I expressed to my friends fourteen years ago, that the farmers of the prairies should take measures to put a good hedge fence round the main lines of their farms, and then, if it was a success, they could make the two main cross fences, which would amount to six hundred and forty rods, which would, to-day, be worth two thousand dollars to every farm having this hedging—and allowing thirty-six sections in a township, at fifteen hundred dollars for each quarter section, would be in value nearly two hundred thousand dollars for the township. Now, admitting one half of the towns in a county to be twelve, these twelve townships would, to-day, be worth over two millions and a half of dollars. With these figures before us, I kindly ask the farmers of the West, and especially the prairie States, to calmly look at this all-important subject of fencing, and see if your prairie farmers by township will not organize, as I have recommended in another place, and adopt measures to secure a good, mellow, dry, rich piece of land, and cultivate the osage orange plants, employing a man to tend them in the best possible manner, and they will be strong thrifty plants; when one year old, they are ready for setting out—you should have the ground, where you design to set your fences, well plowed, twelve inches deep in the fall, and in the spring, as soon as the frost is out, plow the soil over again, have it well harrowed, and make your trench six inches deep—take the plants and cut them down to six inches from the root, take and set your line, setting your plants twelve inches apart, then move the line six inches, and set this row twelve inches apart. Commence by setting the two first plants six inches apart, and afterwards twelve inches, making the plants to stand, when both rows are set, six inches apart from center to center.

In setting the plants out, much care should be taken to have the soil pressed around the plants solid, the soil left two feet each side of the rows, and a little inclined towards the plants, so as to hold the moisture from the showers. During the dry months of July and August, have the plants kept free from weeds, and the second year prune them down to eighteen inches, leaving all the stems below that. The third year cut your top round down to three feet, and you can by the first of June turn it out for a good substantial fence, which has cost you less than one dollar per rod. This is what the farmers want, and what they can have. Put a competent man to take care and see that the plants receive all the attention necessary to insure a first class hedge. By forming a company you make a business of it—and it will cost less than for each farmer to raise his own plants and attend to them himself; but either way, let there be an uprising among the farmers, in view of this grand object. Who can doubt for a moment, the immense wealth it will impart to those who avail themselves of the opportunity of having these splendid green fences, surrounding their farms, say nothing about their two cross fences they are sure to have, as fast as time and means will permit.

My observations taken in Morgan, Sangamon and Knox counties, in Illinois, assures me the safety of the Osage Orange for hedges, and I hope these remarks will find a place in the minds of many farmers, and my greatest pleasure will come, when I know that the farmers of the prairies appreciate these hedges, when they see the prairies of the West enclosed with good live fences, because I feel certain, from all the external evidences, that timber for fencing will inevitably grow dearer, by the increasing demand it must have for building and other purposes. Would it not be well for the farmers who do not feel able to put up temporary fences, to protect their hedges while growing, for two years, to form a union of interest, and mutually agree to take their fences away, and make small fields with them, sufficiently strong to keep what cattle they have. By doing this they will have a free and equal chance to put out their inside division fences, by hedging with Osage Orange, and if you are under the township club organization, all the better, as you have that mutual interest, to make the most money from the least labor expended. You can have a by-law that all damage done by stock, shall be adjusted by the owner. I do not see why this effort should not prove a complete success, and enable all farmers to have a good live fence in three years, that will, with some pruning, last hundreds of years. This, to my mind, is the most feasible way for all farmers to be able to have good fences, made by hedging. Do this by employing one competent man to cultivate the plants, and attend to setting the fence, and all matters pertaining thereto.

Within three years, providing the farmers will make a grand movement in this all important business of completely hedging their farms in the West, I am free to say the mind is not able to compute the immense wealth that in three to five short years will be thrown into the laps of those who cultivate the soil—making the sinews of our country indomitable.

With these remarks on fencing, by hedging, I have made as strong as my mind was able to perform, hoping what I have left unsaid, my farmer friends will perform by actual demonstration, that the best minds of our country will take pride to honor.

P. S. There is a machine already invented, to prune and form the hedge fencing in a splendid manner.

CHAPTER XXIV.

AP'LE CULTURE.

The apple is the substantial fruit of our country, and every farmer in the Eastern, Middle and Western States, and also in the Southern States wherever they will grow, and in the first three sections of our country spoken of above; not one acre of arable land in all these States but what will bear some kind of apples, and according to latitude, climate and soil depends the proper selections of fruits best adapted in every respect to warrant success. When you want to start or replenish your orchard, much discretion should be used in making selections to suit your special locality; but in all localities get some of the most hardy and sure bearers, that you may raise fruit under all circumstances. That is what the farmers want, and that is what they all can have if they will follow my instructions in this essay. During my residence in Maine for twenty years, I never saw an orchard that did not raise more or less fruit every year, and during the time I cultivated the apple in Central Illinois I had some fruit, although they were not set out as they should have been. The last apple trees I transplanted, are bearing very well, and I learn they are growing finely; I took more pains in setting them.

I repeat again that every farmer should have planted, at least, from ten to one hundred trees around his homestead; the soil most sure and suitable for apples is of a clay loam with fine sand, having the proper solidity that will hold the roots by its adhesive strength.

The best location for the orchard is an inclination south-west-south or south-east, but the other points will do, and all of them should have the sheltering care of two rows of cherry or maple trees to the north of your orchard of apples and other fruits, and that should be started immediately, to gain size and grow rapidly the first year. Bear in mind, you have a double purpose with your cherry trees round your fruit orchard, furnishing you good protection and good fruit in cherries of the best varieties. You should have them well planted that they may grow fast, to get a good start the first year.

The plat of ground for your orchard should be well plowed, twelve inches deep, and well manured if the soil is sandy; for plants two years old, the pits should be made, at least, three feet square by two deep. Invert your soil, so as to have the bottom soil to lay around the roots of your trees; if the soil is not rich, your must put more chip, with a mixture of old manure and ashes, or lime well pulverized, with half soil, pack this well round the roots, and, if the soil is not damp, leave the top slightly dishing to hold a little water, when showers come in the dry summer time; put a stake down on the north side of the tree, with a woolen or soft leather band to fasten round the tree to stay it firmly.

Apple trees should be set out from twenty-four to thirty feet apart, in true lines, showing taste, that becomes natural to farmers who take delight in doing their work well at the start, and of course it will always be so if it should stand a hundred years. It would be well to have these pits where you intend setting your trees, made in the fall, laying the dirt in a pile, so that it will shed water well; the frost through the winter will make the soil mellow and friable, and healthy for any plants. Setting should be done as early as possible in the spring, that the roots may take an early start.

The qualities and kinds of trees should be selected with much care. Be sure to take the most thrifty trees of two years from the graft, having well divided roots. If you are starting an orchard, you had better have a few three and four year old trees, and cut off some of the limbs, and if they have good strong roots, they will bear the first year, if you set out well in the fall. The kinds of fruit are numerous, and many choice. Among them are the Winter Baldwins, Spitzenberg, Roxbury Russets, yellow, Belle Flower, Greenings, Peck's Pleasant, Gravenstein, Hubbardston, Nonesuch, Garden Royal, William's Favorite, Ladies' Sweeting, Autumn Sweet, rough, Jersey Sweeting, and the Early Sweet, which are among the choice apples. One of the most hardy and constant bearers is the Wagoner, which should be in every orchard, and not many would be without apples. The Vanderbilt is also an excellent fruit, and will keep well during the winter.

Having your orchard started, I would strictly remind you of the special necessity of having a substantial fence around your garden and fruits. I am sensitive on this point, for I set out my first orchard thirty years ago, having received my trees from Cincinnati, and had to set them without being entirely inclosed; I lost many trees, which was bitter to my feelings. Hence, the farmer should be particular to have his fruits secured, as every tree at one year old is worth five dollars to your farm, and the enhanced value of a well-selected apple-orchard and other fruits is really hard to estimate; but I hazard nothing when I say that you fill up the five acres surrounding your homestead with a garden and choice fruits, and keep, as you should, a short account of all expenses thereto, and the result will show that you have made one hundred per cent. on all money laid out upon the same, and your farm will sell at a higher interest than that; so, friends, you have everything to encourage you onward to complete your fruits as fast as time and means will permit; the only real outlay is the money you invest in the fencing and the cost of the plants, for you can put your labor in at times to advantage, and great pleasure will arise from these labors of cultivating your fruits, adding much to soften the toil of the field labors.

The trees should be mulched in the winter immediately after the first freezing up of the soil, any old straw substance will do, and in the spring, take spade and work this in round the trees with a little lime, chip or old cattle manure, this will give strength to send up food for the apple.

When apples are gathered they should remain in a dry cool place, away from the sun or rain; and kept there as long as the weather will permit—this will put them in a fair condition to keep well through the winter; they require the dryest place in your cellar, and when you are making cider, then comes the special comfort in the long winter evenings to eat these choice apples and drink the cider, with a side bowl of hickory nuts, all of which will conspire to smooth the rough places, and make life what providence designed it should be—a source of pleasure as well as toil.

Trees from the time of setting out, should be pruned, by thinning out all the weakest limbs, and never let one rub or chafe another, and cut back all that seem to be outstripping the others, so as to make the whole tree have a uniform position, and able to bear itself equally from all sides, adding utility by giving it a true balance against the winds, having beauty of symmetry, so essential to distribute the substance to all parts of the tree. Fruits must have plenty of opening left in the top, so that the light, heat and air, can circulate freely, affording life and vigor to the tree, and a richer growth of fruit. This must seem apparent to all, for if the tree retain all the wood it can make, it will furnish room for the juice from the roots, and consequently it supports the limbs, and the fruit will not be able to receive any, or at least but little

Hence the result that thousands of trees bear but little or no fruit in the West. I know they do not look so prolific and pleasing to the eye, but the fruit is better to the taste and stomach, and will make the eyes weep for joy in harmony with their other senses.

All interloping suckers should be cut off whenever they appear; they will not grow much on trees well pruned. I think it would do well to put three peach or pears in the center of your apple trees—have them clustered together and well tended. I think they would pay until the apple trees were large enough to need the room.

Before I dismiss this subject of the apple orchard, I desire to impress this fact upon the minds of the farmers, I mean all who are able to set out ten trees, that the delay of one year in setting out your trees is a delay of much pleasure withheld from your sight in seeing your trees growing, and one year short from fifteen years of seeing your apple trees obtain their full perfection. With all these incentives to stimulate you onward to have more or less of the apple and other delicious fruits growing around you—so pleasant and renovating to sight and feelings, and, above all, healthy to yourself and family. Always lifting the mind away from the gloom that inhabits the breast at times, to higher reflections of happiness, and temporizing the rugged labors of the harvest field, and afflictions that fall in the train of all humanity.

These sentiments are the substance of my own experience, in some measure, while cultivating the soil, and so it is with all professions of industry, to have some prominent feature in their business to strengthen and excite them in their faithful progression to higher and nobler purposes of life, and none need them more than he who cultivates the soil. So, friends, make the trial and progress onward as fast as you can to obtain the rich luxuries there is in the fruits that you can have by making a few extra exertions with the mind, and all will be finished.

CHAPTER XXVI.

BROOM CORN.

The culture of broom corn in the United States has been gradually increasing for the past fifty years, and now it is being extensively cultivated in some of the Western States, and from the prices obtained for good brush will warrant a larger production in the future.

The most available soil for the broom plant to make a good yield is a mixture of sand and clay loam, medium dry and warm soil is the most suitable, and with proper care in its culture, there is no crop grown that will pay the producer a larger profit. But like all other plants, much care is required to insure a large harvest. The soil should be plowed ten inches deep, and well pulverized by the harrow; lay the rows three feet apart with a machine having three shoes, made fast, three feet apart, by two joists, two by six, on these shoes, with pins, and a tongue for the horses to guide it; this will facilitate planting very much, and a machine can easily be made for covering it immediately after dropping, by simply taking,two joists, two by six, twelve feet long, and two small pieces put on to the joists so that they will, in their movement, pass directly on each side of the three rows, having them constructed so that they will cover the seed up well.

In the absence of machines for drilling, this is the most available way for planting, but when you can procure a seed drill it will be still better.

The seed should be well screened from all impurities, and planted not to average less than six inches apart; as soon as the corn is well up, take a fine harrow and care fully cultivate the plants so as to kill all the weeds; the second tending should have a fine cultivator, double, so as to take one row at a time, and the third, the last should be a five teeth cultivator, gauged to dress up the sides of the two rows, leaving the soil a little raised from the plant so as to hold some water from the showers in the dry months of July and August.

At the time when the seed is fully ripe, it should be bent over twelve to eighteen inches below the brush, then let it be well cured before harvesting. The usual way of breaking over the tops is by hand, I would suggest the feasibility of having two men, with light poles from six to eight feet long, to go crosswise of the rows, one on each side, to bare and the other to follow up to press the brush over. It seems to me, when the corn stands, even this would be an excellent way for saving much time and labor, and when well cured, many hands should be employed ready to harvest in the shortest time possible, and handle well, by having it put into the barn or some secure place from all water. Farmers making large crops, would do well to have sheds erected to lay the brush under for safe keeping, and ready for packing into bales. Much care is required to have the brush well laid in the bales, and all the other work should be done in good mechanical order, as no part of the labor attending the culture of broom corn will pay better than making the bales to have good form, and firm, to ship without wastage as it is often done.

It is only a few years that broom corn has been cultivated to any extent in the West, and with proper care to have the soil made friable by deep culture, and it has been under cultivation any length of time, manures should be well incorporated into the soil, with pure seed by screening very closely so as to take out all bad seeds which, if suffered to be sown, will destroy the possibility of having first-class brush; the seed should be sown by drill, or according to the plan I have directed, so as to have the seed pure, planted, of course, at one depth, and it will germinate at once, making an even growth. Lastly, though not least, have the plants cultivated by level culture, leaving the soil, when last tended, slightly inclined to the plants, as I have previously remarked, and none can doubt the result but a full harvest.

CHAPTER XXVII.

PEACH CULTURE.

The peach in some localities in the different States, is extensively raised, and I am aware that the soils and climates of many States are well adapted to grow this most delicious fruit, and the fact ought to insure a lager cultivation. Not doubting the truth of this statement, from my own experience and observations on the peach culture, and having the scenes fresh before my mind, that were exhibited forty years ago in New York City, when the peaches from New Jersey were on sale in the market, well do I remember that Jones' baskets would bring eight dollars, containing half a bushel; of course they were extra choice, and brought out the silver. Well do I also remember the choice peaches I raised in Tazewell County, Illinois, twenty-five years ago, from seed I purchased at Cincinnati and Louisville, having one variety known as Favorite Mellocaton, color deep bright yellow, and very choice flavor. At this time there are very choice peaches growing in Southern Illinois, and the most extensive and justly celebrated place for propagating peaches, is on the eastern shore of Lake Michigan, being in the State of Michigan.

The soil is a mixture of sand and clay, being well adapted for fruit culture, and on the eastern side of the Lake, the weather in the Spring is favorable for the peach crop, and so far as the cities on the Lake with Chicago, are concerned, it is well that peaches will grow there, for the cheap transportation by water is favorable.

Peaches grow well in other parts of Michigan, Illinois, Indiana, Missouri, Iowa, Wisconsin and Minnesota. The great misfortune with the farmers is, their not taking proper measures to cultivate them rightly. It will require some reflection and labor, to have the soil and climate adjusted with the manures, to insure good success in peach culture, and with these aiding facilities, the farmers of the West can have all their families want, and a plenty to spare to towns and cities who are willing to pay good prices for fruits, and consider them a great luxury.

It is well known that vegetables and fruits, are conducive to health, all people, and especially children, are fond of fruits, and sound policy and true economy should impel the farmers to cultivate the peach, with a variety of other fruits, at least for a plentiful supply for home consumption, and whenever they can be easily raised, duty should prompt them to extend their cultivation, to supply those who have not by their occupation, an opportunity to raise them.

How important, then, it is for the farmers of the West to rise up and make one grand universal movement in the fruit culture, testing the soils and climates in an experimental manner, in quantities and qualities, as their better judgment may dictate, from the instruction and best lights shining before you on fruit cultivation.

From my own experience for the past thirty years, and close observations in regard to fruit-growing in the West, I hazard nothing by saying, there is not a single locality in the West where vegetables and plants will grow well, but if proper care and pains are taken in supplying the soil with all the essential food and protection against the elements of winter.

I would recommend the following modes of culture, viz:—On our rich bleak prairies, where the soil has been made rich and porous by the continual burnings of all vegetable substances previous to the time of civilization, and since, leaving the soil, as at present, too light and porous for the entire safety of the roots in the winter time. Hence, to effectually obviate this, the pits for your trees should be taken out twenty-four inches by three feet diameter, then put the bottom soil on the top to set your trees in, doing this work in the fall so that the frost will act on it, then, in the spring, as soon as it will do, take a bushel of half old stock and half old door chip manure, and, thoroughly mixing these together, take your trees—those that have had the strongest growth the previous season—cut off the main stem at the top, and a little off a few branches; this will give the body more vigor to grow and make stronger fruit, put the trees in as solid as they stood in the nursery, with the ground slightly dishing to hold water, so needful to strengthen the plants during the summer months, when the most nourishment is required to make the fruits what they ought to be, rich and nutritious.

Without this process of treatment, and giving a little time and care, as I have directed, you cannot reasonably nor rightly expect to grow fruits to meet your anxious desires. Follow out these instructions, and none can doubt the results of raising fruits on the prairies of the West.

It would be well to have all your fruit grounds made rich by green manure in the fall, and plowed under with a subsoil; this will aid the fruit trees by giving off continually the wholesome gases that proceed from the richly manured grounds, as you would have from such cultivation.

From the strong shelter afforded by your surrounding fruit trees, who can doubt, but with such management, all the farmers of the West can have all the fruits they need from this easy simple labor and much pleasure, by the care you will have to impart to it from time to time, by seeing that weeds are kept away from the roots, taking off all worm and miller nests that may appear upon the trees, and, in very dry times, having a quantity of water pumped up into vessels in the morning, letting it stand in the sun until night, and then putting a few quarts around your trees—this will furnish new life to the young growing fruit that would otherwise perish When the farmers fully realize the living facts that plants, like animals, must have water and food to live and do well, then we shall have a new era in the prosperity of our country's greatness—by the great improvements of our farmers in cultivating the soil on a scientific basis—affording, at less prices, better products from the soil.

By taking the subsoil of our rich prairies and mixing it with manure, as previously stated, you have a soil with sufficient solidity, that neither frost nor dry weather will affect so much, being at all times more strengthening to the roots than top soil under any circumstances whatever ; if you have no chip manure, put in wood ashes, put a ring round your trees eight inches from the tree, this will stop the insects from getting on them, and will aid in giving life to perfect the fruit tree for a vigorous growth to bear choice peaches.

All sand and clay soils, either on the prairie or timber, will grow fruits, and what I desire the farmers to do first, (of course I mean those who have not taken pains to cultivate fruits,) to set off their ground as I have indicated before, and commence with as many trees as their feelings may seem to dictate, and set them as I have directed, in the Spring, as early as the weather will permit. I would cut the top of the main stem some, and a few of the largest branches. This give aid to the balance, and shape the top better. The tree must have stock and substance in the roots and body, if you expect to raise good fruit, and by cropping off some, you have strong, well formed trees. The kinds I would cultivate are the Crawfords, Early Mellocaton, a large rich fruit, strong grower, hardy and popular, and ripens about the first of September. Late Admirable, large size, choice flavor, and is a splendid peach, and is held in high estimation by peach cultivators; as lasting fruit, all will have some of them. Season middle of September.

The President is not so large, but a delicious, very sweet fruit, a healthy, strong grower, very productive. It was first grown on Long Island. Season middle of September.

The Hemskirke is a medium sized, bright orange color, fine juicy rich flavor. A hardy, good bearer, and is highly recommended as a permanent tree to cultivate. Season the last of July.

The Oldmixon, (freestone) is large size, excellent fruit, flesh white, tinged with red, rich and very juicy. None should fail to cultivate this fruit, for it has a full record of good qualities. There are many others I could name, that stand high and grow well in the West, and can be obtained from our best gardens.

Friends, in concluding my remarks on the peach culture, I have only to add, that I truly hope the farmers may feel it their duty to make a movement in starting the fruit garden, even with a few trees, well set out and taken care of, will create a stimulus that will induce all to try their experiments in fruit culture, and in a few years the influence will grow onward until the farmers of the West will think they have no home worth looking at, without fruits growing around it. When that time comes, the farmers will have better health, and prosperity will surely attend them in their onward march to higher and nobler purposes, and mankind will have a National pride for the greater success of the Agriculturalists of our country. Where on earth should we look for more favorable results than in the fertile West, from her rich soil in the hands of worthy farmers, surrounded with increasing millions of inhabitants.

CHAPTER XXVIII.

STRAWBERRY CULTURE.

Why do not the farmers of the West cultivate the healthy and delicious strawberry, having the soil and facilities to do so at their command? But they do not realize how simple the labor is to cultivate and supply their families with this rich luxurious fruit during the entire season which every farmer can and should have at his own home, fresh and pure from the vines. I desire to give the needful information in all its details, so that farmers may learn to know how it can be done, and they will all feel an interest in raising enough for their families, saying nothing about the immense quantities they can raise for the towns and cities, paying them richly for the labor on their production.

SOIL AND PREPARATION.

Any soil in the West that will produce vegetables will grow strawberries, but the best and most reliable soil is a mixture of fine sand and clay; any loamy soil will yield a good return, but manure should be applied on all soils. The soil with the manure must be worked down twelve inches deep, and well pulverized, this will afford nourishment to the young roots, and give vigorous growth to the plants through the entire season; without this full supply of food from the manure, the plants must fail to sustain their bearing qualities, and a short crop will be the result. Hence, the importance of having the soil made mellow, down at least, twelve inches, so that the roots will stretch down and drink up the rich fluid, while the top soil will have been exhausted by the dry weather You can set the plants in rows or hills; if you are only cultivating for family use, the hills are preferable, and when setting, put two plants in a hill six inches apart, and the hills two and a half feet apart each way—setting only the root in the ground, press the soil hard around the roots, leaving the hill a foot diameter, and slightly concave so as to hold a little water from the water-pot or showers. If you cultivate for market, put them in three rows together, twelve inches apart in rows each way, with a space of two and a half feet between the sets of rows, affording room to run the small cultivator. I notice some celebrated cultivators prefer setting these plants in rows, two and a half feet apart and ten inches apart in the rows, but either way will raise good strawberries if they are well cultivated; it would be well to put a little pulverized lime around the roots when setting out, and every spring, when dressing up the soil, you should put on some manure, of a mixture of door yard and cattle, that will strongly nourish the plants for the coming season, and increase the berry and improve the fruit in flavor. Care should be taken in keeping all weeds out; cut the runners off as fast as they appear, which can be done with a light, sharp, narrow hoe; a piece of ground four rods square, well cultivated, will supply your family with all they can use; this is better than an acre badly cultivated.

Farmers, the greatest and most important duties required of those who till the soil is furnishing food to plants, as well as to animals, and the sooner they realize this fact the more certain will prosperity reward all their labors.

There are a large variety of strawberries cultivated, of which I shall mention a few of the most prolific and desirable to cultivate. Care must be taken in making the best selections, as there is quite a difference in their qualities and production, I would recommend for early use Burr's New Pine, Baltimore Scarlet, Jennie Lind and Russell's. For the choice later varieties, take, over all others, for present culture, the Triomphe de Gand, Wilson's Albany and the Crimson Green. But with all these, there are new varieties being propagated yearly, and it would be well to try a few of these new kinds as an experiment; you will have plenty of strawberries if you take a little pains to keep weeds and runners out of the way, and you will have the delicious fruit that all so much admire.

The strawberry is a sensitive plant, easily affected by good or bad culture; hence, it requires the soil to be kept free of weeds, and lightly dressed, with the soil raised a little round the plants for dry weather. For winter clothing to keep the plants warm and healthy, go to the timber and get leaves to spread over the beds, and it would be well before the hard freezing, to put on some rye or oat straw, which gives sure protection. As soon as it will do in the spring, take off the straw, and let part of the leaves remain around the roots, spreading on a little old manure; take a four teeth iron rake and work the manure in with the leaves, and it will have a good effect to give the plants an early start. So you will have no more trouble than to keep the runners off, and the result will be, for this little amount of labor that all farmers can spare, and from June till September the cultivators of the soil, yes, the farmers, who so nobly work in the dust, they can have their rich strawberries and cream, from their own raising not once a week or month when they go to town, but they can have them daily fresh, with all the cream they want, not sour, nor wilted strawberries as you may often find at the restaurants. Farmers, I do not think it is necessary for me at this time to urge you on to cultivate these delicious fruits, so healthful when fresh, for I think you will catch the strawberry fever, that no physician will be able to cure until you take the strawberry lozenges, so rich and aromatic to the taste. I know there are some farmers that cultivate this rich fruit, but where there is one that does, there are a hundred that do not. I am unselfish in this business, and want all to enjoy the pleasures that are so easily obtained by a little sweet labor, say nothing of the pleasure realized.

Now, friends, in closing my remarks on the strawberry culture, I desire to draw a picture, the design to be a front view of a farmer's home, taken in July, one hour to sunset, when they rays will reflect life and beauty upon the surroundings of that center, where the farmer sits with his family in that bower of evergreens and flowers, faring sumptuously over their delicious Triomphe de Gand, strawberries and cream.

Let all carry out the plans I have suggested and presented for your consideration on the strawberry culture, and the artist will have thousands of just such real literal scenes as the farmers home in the West, which I have feebly represented to you with my pen. But, in a word, I truly hope you will respond by action! action! and none can doubt the final result.

CHAPTER XXIX.

GRAPE CULTURE.

The history of the grape has a date back to the early existence of man. Was first cultivated in Asia and Persia, and thence through all the countries of the Eastern Hemisphere. The berries were fermented, and a beverage was made with fair success. It is reported that Noah cultivated the grape vine in Palestine, two thousand three hundred and fifty years before Christ, and nations acquired them from nations, and they were brought to our country by its early settlers. They can be cultivated successfully in a large portion of the United States, and by acclimation, I think it will find soil and climate to produce some varieties of choice fruits over our whole country, and especially the Western States, with proper culture, will be suscepti-ble of bearing large quantities of choice, rich flavored grapes.

It is conceded that cattle manures, mixed with oat or barley straw litter, is the most congenial organic substance, to make the plants grow in a healthy condition; it must be well stirred up with the soil, and when the soil is destitute of lime, it must be supplied with ashes or lime, well pulverized with the soil around the

roots. A fine, sandy, clay loam, having an elastic substance, from my experience and observation, is the most suitable for grape culture, but any medium dry soil, made rich and full of strength, so essential to produce that richness grapes must have to be choice. The soil should be kept free from all weeds, and raise the soil around the plants after the Spring rains have passed, so that the soil will hold some water from the showers, and if there should be a dry time through the Summer, care should be taken to have water drawn from the well in the morning into casks, and let it stand until night, when it can be sprinkled around the roots. It would be well to add a few wood ashes, to give the soil an alkalescent tone, to keep up a vigorous growth for the plants through the dry season. Without this application of water, the fruit cannot be nutritious in substance, and the product will be light and poor. Without this special care in your culture of the grape, you had better let them alone.

The proper time to commence working the soil is in the Spring, when the frost has passed, and the warm air is penetrating the roots of the vines; in dry mellow soil deep cultivation is best, and moisture is necessary to insure a strong growth to the vines; but if the soil is solid, cold and wet, much chip manure and lime or ashes should be thoroughly worked in around the roots every spring, as extra means to give this cold soil a healthy tone to create the true elements that must exist to warrant a good production. With care and attention to keep the vines in their proper places through the season, there ought to be a good yield of fruit. When you intend starting a plot of ground for grape culture, or where you have done so, you should, in the Fall, subsoil your ground sixteen inches deep, and put into the trenches a mixture of straw and fresh cattle manure, which contain less nitrogen than other manures, hence, the better for grapes; you can also add with this manure the straw of bean, pea, or oat, all being well charged with alkaline substance, so essential to grape culture.

The proper time for harvesting is when the clusters hang down heavily and the stems are becoming hard and woody, and when the juice has acquired its natural vinous flavor with its saccharine substances predominating, then it is, according to the most experienced cultivators, the most suitable time to save your fruits.

For wine purposes, it is well to let them remain on the vines as late as possible without the frost hurting them, although a little frost may seem to help them. As to the practical experience and proper labor to be used in making wine, I respectfully refer you to the most able and elaborate writings of Professor Longworth of Cincinnati, who has labored long and faithfully, with untiring zeal, to bring the culture of grapes up to its present state of perfection, and it is conclusive evidence, by his unbounded success, that the culture of grape is very profitable, and I would commend and urge every farmer to cultivate grapes, either as an investment to make money by selling the grapes to the thousands of people who cannot raise them from their

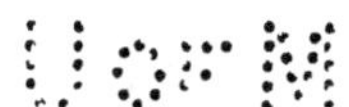

occupations of life, or manufacture them into wine. And last, though not least in one sense, I would earnestly recommend you to raise them for the special blessings they afford your family, who, above all on earth, are first entitled to eat them, for their luxury and health. What surprises me most is to find that there are more fruits eaten in the towns and cities than by the farmers, in proportion to the number of inhabitants. I would ask the question, why is it; are the people in the cities better able to eat them? certainly not—do they taste better to them than they do to those who have the soil, and with little trouble can raise them?—it would seem not; then we only assign it as a reason why the farmers, as a mass, have not realized the great blessings there are in raising fruits for themselves, with plenty to spare, so that all the people may feast upon them, is because they think they cannot spare the time from their heavy labors of cultivating the crops; this is a wrong impression, and the sooner they take a little time to raise some of the different kinds of fruits, the more pleasure and health will they enjoy. The Delaware, Clinton, Concord, Catawba, Herbemont and Elsinburgs are among the first for successful cultivation, and the most reliable —with many other varieties the farmers can always make fine selections; I also recommend the Black Hamburgh as a superior fruit, and they are successfully cultivated in the gardens of Chicago, by our wealthy citizens. They have been sold in this market as high as two dollars per pound.

MODE OF PLANTING GRAPES.

The rows should run North and South, that the sun, through the middle of the day, will shine through the length of the rows. If you design only to cultivate a small piece of ground in your garden, I would put it in an arbor form, having the first say eighteen inches from the ground, and so on up to the top, setting the plants from four to six feet apart. I should prefer the one year old plants, the roots are more fibrous, do not suffer so much in transplanting, and, with care, will take vigorous start and bear fruit as soon. Very little danger is apprehended about their not living.

After the first year, you can procure your own cuttings from the vines you have growing, and as soon as the vines have done growing in the fall and are at rest, you can begin to train your vines; the object of pruning is to regulate the growth and bearing of the vine, by cutting all shoots and branches that obstruct the true development of the vine for its future prosperity in order to perfect its fruit. Beginning with plants two years old, they are pruned back again to one or two eyes, this will form a head from which emanates more or less sprouts every year, allow these to grow through the season, and when strong to bear, two or three of these sprouts are pruned to spurs of having two or three eyes and all the rest cut off.

If you desire to extend your grapery, you can put up trellis work with posts and light bands of wood tastefully built, so as to hold your vines in a secure manner. I see some persons are putting up wire of the size of telegraph—its utility I cannot decide. At the same time this trellis work is being finished, the grapes are bearing. With the Summer pruning, all unnecessary growth should be cut away, only those shoots should be allowed to grow which will make bearing wood for the next year.

The trellis covering for the grapes is a prevention of the mildew; it would be well to experiment, to test that important feature in grape culture.

In the fall, the growth for the past season should be cut back, leaving only one or two eyes, and if there are shoots having borne fruit on the second year's growth, cut them off altogether, allowing the plant to get strength of root and wood that will bear choice fruit the next year.

The most important point in grape culture is to have the roots go deep into the soil; hence, as I said before, they should be made rich with manures and deeply pulverized, so essential to give all the life and strength of food the plants must have in order to give a rich harvest, and let me tell those of my friends who will take hold of the delicious grape culture, that the great and all-important secret in having success, is, first prepare your ground well in the fall, as described in this essay, and, with wonted industry, I am fully assured, that if I could be favored to make a call at your residence the second year of your experiment of fruit culture, I would find some of, I do not care which, only to know they were from the origin of the same grapes that were pressed at an early day by the best man the world's history has on record. Who will be the first to respond and add this feature to the surroundings of their pleasant homes?

In conclusion, I will briefly say that the grape culture is an inexhaustable source of pleasant labor, and all who have taste for such should make experimental trials in propagating the native seedlings, and cross them with the well-known hardy kinds and choice in flavor, and in a few years, you have succeeded in bringing out a new species, surpassing any kind on record, and I would strongly recommend all who like the grape culture to go to the forests having the wild vines and set a number of roots out and cultivate them, from such you can make choice selections for hybridizing with the most approved varieties.

But the most available method to sustain and perpetuate the hardy rich varieties, is from the native seed, from the wild plants of the forests that have a thrifty, hardy appearance. Any farmer or gardener who has an inherent taste for fruit culture has a large field opened to him and all who may desire to become amteurs; and who shall succeed in obtaining the highest flavors and improved varieties, will receive a rich reward to themselves and lasting benefit to mankind. I commend this most worthy enterprise to all the farmers of the West, and hope a large number will be found, if not to propagate the fruits themselves, will encourage those who have a desire to do so, by liberally taking plants from those who are and will cultivate the best fruits for the climates and soils of our whole country, and the largest mind cannot comprehend all its future benefits.

In conclusion, let me remind those who cultivate fruits, that they must have patience and perseverence to accomplish and gratify all their wishes, and if one quarter of what they plant produce fruit, they are richly paid for all their labors, and doubly so, taking the pleasures into account.

CHAPTER XXX.

RASPBERRY CULTURE.

The Raspberry is a very choice flavored fruit, and is always ready to take the place of the delicious strawberry on its timely departure from its many votaries, in fact the earliest one on hand before the Strawberries are all gone.

How kind in our beneficent Creator and supplier of all things, to have these precious fruits come so regular in rotation, affording his people lasting pleasures in feasting on the rich vegetables and fruits throughout the entire year.

How can the farmer, having all the facilities to furnish himself and family, withhold his hands from taking an active part in cultivating at least a few of these most delicious, health-giving fruits. All it wants to accomplish these great blessings, is a willing mind to take the first step, and no danger of the result.

The raspberry is one of the best, and very easily cultivated. Any soil having a mixture of sand and clay, or loamy land will bear raspberries, no matter if it inclines to the North; in dry weather the hot sun does not effect them so much. On heavy rich prairies, I would take up the sub-soil, consisting of a clay loam, and rest it on the top, and by manuring this well with cattle and chip manure, well pulverized together, down fifteen inches.

Planting should be done early in the Spring, as soon as the weather will permit. To insure a good start, take the one year old strong plants. Much care should be taken to set them in fresh stirred soil, and only cover up the roots well with mellow soil, made rich and strengthening, to give the plant a strong growth the first year. Pinch off the bearing buds the first season, in order to give more strength to the cane for the second year's growth.

If your soil is rich, put your plants six feet each way, put down three stakes to each plant in the Fall. During the first two years you can raise peas or beans in rows, so you can cultivate the raspberries at the same time you do the beans or peas. Be sure to keep the plants free from all weeds, and after May, raise the dirt around the plants, so as to hold water from the showers, and in a very dry time take well water, draw it in the morning, and let it stand until night; wet the soil around the plants; this will keep up a growth of the fruits, when oftentimes, without this sprinkling, the fruit must perish.

The true policy is to have a well in the middle of the garden, with a force pump and hose, to force the water up into a reservoir. With a hose this water can be carried over all the plants in the garden, saving much time and trouble, enough to pay a large interest, for the daughters and even the wife can hold this hose very nicely for nourishing the delicious fruits.

There are different opinions as to the best time for pruning. Some say the Fall, after the fruit is taken off, and others say early in the Spring, which time, I think is best to prune them, from the fact the wounds inflicted suffer more in the Fall on account of the weather, than they will in the Spring, when the warm weather is starting all vegetation into active life.

Care should be taken to cut off all the slender and most weakly stalks, leaving only four or five in a hill. As I have said before, make the soil strong with food to nourish the plants to insure a full harvest.

MOST RELIABLE KINDS.

There are many names for the raspberry, and, like other berries, much interest is taken to propagate and bring out new kinds as an improvement upon the old names, and as fast as they are established and made known to be the best, the people of course will procure them. The most reliable kinds that people have confidence in are the Antwerp, Hudson River, American Red, called by some the Purple Cane, which is a very choice fruit and a good bearer, the Hornet, Cataioissa, Brinkle's Orange, Franconia and Knevett's Giant are among the best, and I would recommend the farmers to try a few of these, taking the Red or Purple Cane and the Red Antwerp; but if there are any others that have a better record, why, take them, and if but a few, be sure to take the little pains required to make them produce a good yield, and you will enjoy the rich fruits for your labor rendered, then you will have another valuable feature strongly set in the surroundings of your home, stimulating you onward to greater and higher efforts to adorn the worthy profession of cultivating the soil of our country.

CHAPTER XXXI.

OTHER FRUITS NECESSARY TO CULTIVATE.

THE QUINCE

Is a desirable fruit for rich preserves, and is easily cultivated. Soil that will grow the pear will produce the quince. Get the hardy plants, and prune them back first two years, so as to get more strength in the body, so essential to produce good sound fruit, for a shriveled quince is worthless.

THE SIBERIAN CRAB APPLE

Is one of the best fruits for making good rich preserves for common use, and especially with buckwheat cakes. Same kind of soil as other fruits, and the same cultivation. It is a hardy plant and very constant bearer. You should have a few of these trees, and you will not regret the trouble and little expense after having tried them one season.

THE BLACKBERRY

Is much admired for its healthful, rich flavor. Large quantities in some parts of our country are growing wild, and are largely gathered for the rich puddings and pies they will make. In some parts of our country, they are quite extensively cultivated, and large quantities are dried for the pie and pudding through the year. Where the raspberry will grow, there you can have the blackberry. All farmers should have this fruit. What delicious fruit they are for tea, and for a few hour's labor only, all can have them, if they will go to the barrens, where they grow wild, and take up a load of the best young plants; take up some soil with them, and set them out well early in the Spring. Cut off the tops, and set them the same as the raspberry. By pruning and cultivating these wild plants, you can have improved fruit. The object is well worthy the experiment, and by setting out some of the wild with those that have been cultivated, they will unite and produce some choice fruits. My advice is to try the experiment, and you will see the result, to your great satisfaction.

THE CHERRY.

There are several very celebrated kinds of cherries that are cultivated in our country with great success—they are the most hardy fruit cultivated, and always find ready sale for eating in their raw state, and for the rich pudding and pie they will make for your first fruit in June—they will serve you a double purpose, besides giving you rich fruit, they will also afford a good shelter for all your other fruits, so essential in winter. The choicest and most reliable kinds are the Reine Hortense, the Black Tartarian, the Early Richmond, the Red Jacket, and Belle de Choisy. I would recommend the farmers to purchase quite a large number of these trees, and set them about six feet from the fence, as described in my diagram of the home and surroundings; this distance will prevent outsiders from picking them off from the outside of the fence, while the trees will help to form a shelter for your inside fruit; these plants can be obtained at any of the celebrated nurseries in the West.

Take the young hardy plants instead of the older trees that have been stunted in their growth. A word to the wise is sufficient on this subject—I will only say be sure and have these plants growing as soon as time will warrant their transplanting, which is best in the Spring.

THE GOOSEBERRY.

This is an early fruit, and will pay to have a few plants, they are very prolific and serve well for early sauce. You can have them in May—they are about the first green fruit you can have by natural cultivation—try a few of them for a change, they make a good pie or pudding

The best kinds are the Washington Seedlings, Keepsake, Bunker Hill, Governors, Abraham Newland, Green Prolific and the Patterson Seedling. They are easily tended, by keeping the weeds away from the roots through the Summer, and in the Fall, take out one half the roots of the oldest, and place in around the roots some manure, covering it over with the soil you have taken out.

THE CURRANT.

Currants are fine berries, and if well cultivated, come early in June; they should be set out with only one stock in a place, set them three feet apart in rows, make the soil deep and mellow, have it rich with any kind of manure, cultivate them the same as corn, and by having them grow on the single stalk in a place, they will be very large and fine for the table, and, by labor, will make excellent wine. One acre of currants well tended will produce one hundred bushels of fruit; the large red for all purposes, but the white are very choice for table use, and farmers will do well to have these included in their catalogue of fruits.

CHAPTER XXXII.

SORGHUM CULTURE.

There are but two kinds cultivated in the Northern States, viz: the African and the Chinese, and by mixing the seed in some localities, the pure of either kind are hard to obtain. Since the first introduction of the plants into the United States, I have watched, with great interest, the success and prosperity of their culture and qualities, and it is conceded the African, or Impee, is the most preferable, having a more vigorous growth, and its juices are richer and more limpid, showing one degree richer in sugar; hence, the African cane has the preference.

SOILS AND TIME OF PLANTING.

Strong, warm, rich, friable soil is the best, and more certain to grow a sound crop, on account of its early ripening, you should never plant on wet soil; deep plowing, and well pulverized with pure seed, must insure a good harvest. Planting depends upon the season, and the condition of the soil, therefore, I would plant as soon as the weather will permit the ground to be sufficiently dry; the seed should be soaked in warm water until germination is perceptable, this will take two days for the Impee and four for the Sorghum seed. I would cultivate the rows North and South, letting in more light and heat; some claim the preference to plant East and West on account of saving the heavy winds, which would seem to be the best. But the body of the cane would hold a hard wind, and if the situation of the land is high it would perhaps be the safest way to plant it, in good soil, four feet apart, and the seed not under six inches, if possible, in the rows.

CULTIVATION.

The young plant when first up is very small, hence, much care is required to have the harrow take out the small weeds around it, the second tending should be cultivation, to stir the soil well so as to kill all weeds and leave the soil level, so that the showers will get in around the roots in dry weather. When they do come, if the suckers show too much growth they should be cut off, so as to give the main plant a good chance to make a large growth; if the suckers were allowed to be harvested with the cane, they will more or less impart a grassy flavor, and create a little acid, which detracts from the assurance of making good sugar.

The time to commence cutting depends much on the season, as to the weather being more or less favorable for maturing the plant; but as soon as the frost has struck the foliage and seed tufts, the sooner the cane is trimmed of the leaves and top cut off to three feet the better, which, if saved well, will make good feed for stock. The cane should be cut near the ground, and thirty to forty stalks should be shocked together and tied up strong with two bands from the wilted leaves, then, in a short time, if you are not ready to commence crushing your cane, you should haul this up and have it put under shelter and kept some weeks; such keeping adds to the flavor of the juice and saccharine richness very much.

Care should be taken, if possible, not to have a hard frost come on the cane while standing; if, however, such should be the case, all despatch should be rendered to have the cane run through the mill, for if a warm sun should strike on the cane, fermentation would set in, and much danger of spoiling the best part of your crop.

In reference to the best machines and modes of superior manufacture, I would refer you to those who are more acquainted with the business. But follow out the ways I have recommended in the culture, and I feel assured you will have a large harvest.

CHAPTER XXXIII.

CULTIVATION OF THE PEAR.

THE SOIL AND ITS PREPARATION.

The pear is one of the most unattractive plants, as it stands in its own native forests of Asia, and it would seem barely possible that such a sour distasteful fruit could have ever been cultivated and propagated up to produce such delicious and wholesome fruit, as we find is being raised to some extent in the United States. It was cultivated a hundred years ago, in the state of New York, and well do I remember those old and stately pear trees that stood in and around the city of New York over forty years ago, and one especially known as the Stuyvesant tree, celebrated for its venerable cast, say nothing of its rich fruit, and nearly where the heart of the city stands to-day.

They were cultivated quite extensively on Long Island at that time, by the Dutch, but not such fine flavored as now, and when I see how much improvement has been made, in varieties and qualities, I am surprised they are not propagated and urged forward more by the Horticulturists, so that every gardener and farmer in our country shall have them growing, for they can be cultivated on all table land in the West. Sand and clay loam is the best, and on our dry rich prairies, they can be cultivated to do well, by a little extra labor in digging the pit holes three feet by two deep, inverting the soil. Peform this labor in the Fall, so as to have the frost act upon it well for Spring. As soon as the frost is out, and your ground dry enough, take a bushel of old barn and chip manure, and mix it well in with the top soil, where you have it ready for setting. Before setting, I would puddle the roots in rain water with the same soil, this will give the roots fresh life, ready to start with vigor in their new habitation; much care is needed to see that the dirt is pressed around all the roots while setting—put the roots down on the quince stock three inches, not so much on its own standard; have them stand ten feet apart each way, with a stake at the north side, and fasten with a woollen cloth around the tree to hold the sway of the wind.

KINDS AND MODE OF CULTURE.

There are quite a large number of different kinds; the Bartlett, I believe, stands, in all respects, over all qualities—I will here name Beurre D'Anjou, Seckel, Lucrative, Beurre Bosc, Lawrence, Winter Nelis, Dogenne, Louise Bonne D'Jersey, etc. But out of this number I would take four Bartletts, to one Seckel, one Beurre Bosc, and to one Urbaniste, these are the best to start on, being the most reliable of those which I have named. The Bartlett should be planted on the pear root; with proper care, however, it will do well on the quince root. It should not be permitted to ripen in large crops when young. The Urbaniste is a healthy tree, yet it is a long time coming into bearing, but on the quince, the fruit is very excellent and suitable to harvest in October.

The Dogenne Gray is a large rich pear, and will grow well on the quince root, these few samples I have mentioned, will do well to start on.

The manner of culture, is to follow out my suggestions, and if your land is level and inclined to be wet, in order that you may cultivate a few pears, I would recommend the plow, and ridge your ground up and drain off the water, so as to make the soil as friable as possible, in this case I would advise you to go to the dry barrens and get a load of the top mould and mix this with the old manures from the door and cattle yards; put one bushel of this to one bushel of mould from the timber, and set your trees out with care, packing this mixture well around the roots; by this management, if the ground is cool and damp, you can cultivate what few pears you may want for your own use; by trying a few you can see how they will grow.

Keep the ground free from all weeds, and the soil cultivated and raised a little around the trees to hold water when the showers fall through the summer, this must be attended to in order to have your trees do well. Wash the trunks of the trees once in two weeks with soap suds, adding some wood ashes and salt, this will eradicate the insects that infest the trees at times. This washing will give life and vigor to the trees, and pay you well for your labor. In the Fall, after the ground is a little frozen, have all the fruit trees well mulched with leaves from the timber and rye or oat straw; put the leaves on first and then straw—if five feet round, the better for the safety of the trees—let part of this mulching remain the following season, to keep the weeds away and give nourishment to the roots, which is as essential to plants as animals.

Friends, in conclusion, let me say that it is not the quantity, but the quality that I advise you to cultivate, and how to do it. My great desire is that you may raise some of the kinds I have named, and others, to try their qualities; do this and you will fill up the surroundings of that home, adding another chain of attachment which will hold all the stronger in future time.

SUPPLEMENT.

MAKING PURE BUTTER.

In reviewing my manuscript on the dairy, I find, in reference to the essential ways and means to be carried out for its sure preservation, I was not as full and explicit as I should have been, hence, I feel it incumbent on me to extend my remarks on that part of the subject; but first, I will briefly repeat what I have said and written many times, that the main substance for making pure butter and cheese is in having good cows, that give an even quality of milk, and if the farmers have any cows that give poor milk, sell them to the butchers, for one cow that gives a lifeless-colored milk will injure the pure colors of five.

PRESERVATION.

Preservation means and includes all the necessary pre-requisites attending the entire dairy business, but the most trying and difficult part of all is to churn the cream when it has its proper temperature, so that it will give up in good time all the rich substances which the cream contains to make pure butter.

Now, instead of taking the butter out in its pure state by the hands, and working it over some time to get the buttermilk out by washing it with water by the hands, imparting carbonic acid gas, so poisonous to the well keeping of pure butter, I propose to offer my views in regard to the safest and surest way to free the butter from the buttermilk and keep it as pure as it came from the churn. Thus, in the first place, dairymen who assume and want to make pure butter that will keep sweet through the year, must have a churn in the form of a barrel, with floats on the sides and a cylinder in the center, somewhat like Davis' Churn, that will materially assist in separating the buttermilk, after the butter has effectually come, start the plug at the bottom of the churn and quietly revolve the cylinder until you can scarcely see any buttermilk coming away. Then take two large dipper wooden ladles, made expressly for that purpose, and take the butter out on to a table with grooves cut on the top, which will allow the milk to pass off freely. Then have a comb, made of wood, with a head two inches square, and set teeth made one inch broad, in an oval form, twelve inches long, so you will have five inches on each side of the head, and by having these teeth made one end larger, and the other end smaller, so that you can gently pass it through the butter; change it alternately, it will then more effectually let off the milk from the butter by passing down the avenues these teeth will make. With this improvement, let the table be inclined as much as practicable to allow the milk to run off readily, and by the lever which is attached to your table, have the press board large enough to cover all the butter on the table. Have also a cushion made of cotton cloth fastened to your press board, so that while you are working the butter with the comb. or butter preserver, you can quietly press down your cushion, thus, in a very short time, the buttermilk will be all out, and the globules of butter, slightly inclosed in the white casein, which will hold them, by this gentle treatment, in their natural form, so necessary to keep the butter in its purity for any length of time. Then take the butter from the table with the large butter ladle, and put it into the tub, previously working in with the preserver, add one half ounce of salt to a pound of butter, which you have weighed by the scales you have on hand. Be sure to have in your butter tub a resting board, raised in the middle, with grooves and half inch holes, so as to let off any liquid that may possibly remain in the butter, then set it away in your cool butter cellar, where you must let it remain twelve hours, then take and put it on your table, and roll it out with your cushioned roller, then take the seive and put on salt enough to make an ounce clear after what you have worked out of the butter. Then having had the firkins well saturated with brine—pack your butter with a wooden screw, set in a frame for that purpose, put a follower on the butter when you press it, having it also cushioned. By this process, your butter is made and packed without having the grain and rich globules of the butter broken.

In the composition of butter as a whole, we find, when manufactured, more excitable matter therein contained, than in any other substance of the same weight for food. Hence, how very important to have it made pure from all that would have a tendency to corrupt it in the least. So truthful is this the case, that if any feature is withheld from the current of its progress—from the change of cows-food, manner of keeping the milk, temperature, and so on throngh its various stages until it comes to salting. Here is a stand point, that dairymen, whether small or large, are required to unite in sentiment and action, irrespective of all interests and prejudices that may dwell in any dairyman's mind, in regard to this or that salt as having been used. Come square down and resolve, one and all, not to purchase from any salt dealer or merchant, any dairy salt, unless they are willing to guarantee it to be the Ashton or the pure Onondago dairy salt, having the assurance that it is from their lawful agents. I know the Ashton salt is good for butter, as I have used it when in the dairy business, and from the examination I have made with the two kinds. I cannot tell the difference; they seem to have nearly one complexion of clearness and solidity of strength in power of dissolution, and from the representation of C. Comstock, the Onondago Salt Company's agent at Chicago, I learn that the Company have put into their works two mills, with machinery costing seventy-five thousand dollars each, for the sole purpose of preparing the dairy salt upon a scientific chemical basis, whereby all impurities are extracted, which precludes all possibility of lime or any other substance remaining in the salt to injure butter.

Now, friends of the dairy, it would seem vague and useless for me to urge you, who are now in this business, about pure salt, but I am informed by Mr. C. Comstock that he has sold three times as much of his second quality of dairy salt as he has of the first and pure; one costing three dollars and seventy-five cents per barrel, and the pure, five dollars in sacks all in barrels. A small item when one pound will salt sixteen pounds of butter—only one cent and a quarter difference on the sixteen pounds. Now, my advice on this all important subject is for the dairyman not to purchase any other than the pure from the merchants, for their dairy and family table use, then you cannot have it mixed. For without pure salt, free from lime and other impurities, the dairyman cannot make good butter, if he has all other features as perfect as the art of man could possibly make them, all would pass for naught as far as good butter was concerned.

WASHING BUTTER WITH WATER

Should never be indulged in by dairymen, and more especially if it is made for long keeping, from the fact that water is highly charged with oxygen, and all the particles of butter come directly in contact with the water full of oxygen of the atmosphere, much more than if the butter was all pressed out by a cushioned press and rollers—saving the butter in a more perfect manner by not having the grain broken nor injured by impure water being saturated through it, which must promote decomposition of the butter and prevent it from keeping well. Hence, I desire the farmers will give the plans I have suggested a fair trial; I would also give the two best qualities of dairy salt a fair experimental trial, by packing two firkins, dividing the same butter with the Onondago and the Ashton, putting into the firkins the same quantities of each, and, of course, the best the dairymen want and must have, to make good butter. It would be well to have some rock salt with which you can soak your firkins some days before packing; this will take out all impurities that may be in the wood. Make the press-board twelve inches square, round the edges and corners. The cushion should be of sleazy white cotton cloth, in a strip twelve feet long and the width of the press-board, with two straps at each end to keep it in place; after using it, have it well washed and dried. Have the same material and length on the roller, which should be two feet long by four inches diameter. With these appliances all made and kept in perfect order, the means of having pure sweet butter will manifest itself when the process is effectually carried out.

Let this rest upon your minds, one and all, and you, as dairymen, will have the pleasure of making good butter to reward you in a double sense—the mind and pocket, which never can go back on you.

There never was a time in the history of our country, when the dairy business would pay better than now, and all it wants is a taste for the business, with the locality of soil for sweet grasses and pure water, and having the taste and industry to carry out all the leading features laid down in my writings on the dairy business, will my prediction, made in another place, be sustained, that the Northwest, within ten years, will be justly claimed the head quarters for raising the dairy standard to the highest elevation in the world. So trim your lamps for more light, and the day is sure to dawn upon your efforts by the final result.

OMISSIONS AND ITEMS WORTHY OF NOTE.

All farmers should have from forty to one hundred and sixty rods of moveable fences on their farms, so available to partition off fields, in pastures, meadows, and grazing for stock, etc.

Without pure sound seed planted, your labors are lost and hopes blasted.

The more perfect are your farming implements, the larger will be your harvest.

Good treatment to your domestic animals is better than gold at compound interest.

Remember that a rotten rail, stake, board or post holds your products in danger.

Always have food enough on hand for your stock without being obliged to turn them on your fields when the ground is soft.

Water, the purest and most plentiful, has the first and highest value for a good farm.

All needful tools for farming should be procured at times when they are not specially wanted.

The smallest products come from the largest farms for the labor rendered.

The cheapest articles of implements and stock are the dearest in the end.

One day's labor expended in preparing your seeds, for safe keeping until they are sown, is worth fifty at common labor.

Better pay three prices for seeds best adapted to your soil, than to sow those that are otherwise.

When you ascertain how much weight you can put on an animal in ten days by good regular feeding, it will show and prompt you to put on as much in proportion for one hundred days.

Feed the soil with rich food, and the plants will furnish the same to the animal.

If one tree will bear fruit, you have an evidence that more can be made to bear with it.

It is more pleasant and desirable to look after work that is before you than that which is behind

Fortunes have been made from five minutes reflection, wisely directed

Bedding, for resting your grain or hay upon, should be made in sections as fencing, and will serve you eight months for that purpose.

Draining lands that are moist and wet, is the best endowment the farmers can make, to sustain the highest interests of agriculture.

There is no telling how much the farmer will gain by reading this book, until he shall have practiced and carried out the precepts therein contained.

Now, Friends—Farmers of the West, this is the end of the beginning; but, I hope, not the end of the last.

DISTRIBUTION OF TIME.

The distribution of time for the laboring classes of our country, has brought the progressive mind into requisition from time to time, just as fast as civilization, education, and the mechanic arts have advanced, have we found the burdens of the laboring classes made lighter. From the fourteen hour system down to twelve, and from that down to ten hours. And now under the rapid advancement of intellectual knowledge, with the laborers of our country, and the extensive improvements made in all kinds of labor-saving machinery, both for manufacturers and farmers, would seem to warrant another reduction of two hours,—making eight hours for all the regular laboring men, who work by the day faithfully, shall constitute the requirements, by the employers, from the employes, for their day's labor. Let this arrangement be perfected between the parties so inseperably interested, that one cannot subsist and exist without the other. Hence the stronger these facts are manifested and exemplified by the employer and employe, the more sure will peace and prosperity prevail throughout our entire country. The minds of our State and National Legislatures are being moved in relation to this momentous subject, and the State of Illinois has passed a law to that effect, and it is hoped and believed the law will be cheerfully sustained. But as to its being satisfactorily acquiesced in by the employers, will very much depend upon the faithful and earnest manner the employes perform their labor during these eight hours. Here I will remark from my own experience of thirty years, having had occasion to employ from five to fifty hands, and the shortest time made with them was eight hours, and I never had my work more faithfully done, and as much done as though they had worked the ten hours. The cause for this is obvious, from the fact they knew they were saving two hours time, and they worked with a will, not taking up their time with idle talk, and I have no doubt but a large majority of the operatives will look at it in this light, and give entire satisfaction to their employers.

Now, if this measure is adopted and carried out, in the spirit it ought to be, and as all philanthropists desire it should, the fruits will be shared equally alike with the employed and employer, for without this generous feeling existing between them, the fruits of their labor will never be as full and rich. Hence, I say again, strike hands in all the States that adopt the eight hour rule, and let the employes go to work and make their eight hours' labor show that they can do as much by close attention to their business, as they would have done on the ten hour rule, and better workmanship, by specially minding what they are doing; let this be your aim, whether you are farming or making farmers' implements, or any other machinery, for labor is work, and if any laborer need relief it is him who cultivates the soil. In behalf of their interests, I will here state what I think, after much reflection, should be their rule of action — thus: Adopt the eight hour rule for actual labor in the field, clear from taking care of your teams, and divide the twenty-four hours in the following manner, to wit: eight hours to labor, eight hours to sleep, four hours to improve the mind with suitable books, and four hours for recreation, all to be done with moderation. Fill the time in all its several parts, faithfully, for one month, and I feel confident you never will return to the old habit of making sixteen hours for your day's labor, as I have done many a day with the farmers of Illinois. It is true, while you have these eight hours for rest and eating your meals, you can look at the best works on Agriculture, so as to keep your farming interests before you, so that what you may plant or sow, the increase will give rich reward, showing that the head has labored with the hands. I think it would be well for the farmers, when they adopt the eight hour system, in summer, to divide the time, as follows: work from seven to eleven—rest three hours, until two, then work till six, you having three hours until nine, for reading and improving the mind. Keep a record of daily events, and you will find it both profitable and pleasant, and will not regret it.

With these passing remarks on the subject of labor, I place them at the close of my book, and truly hope the farmers of the West will find it to be their special interest to give the sentiments in regard to labor a fair experimental trial, in all its bearings, and the result will show whether it will stand or fall.

Your Friend,

FOLSOM DORSETT.

www.ingramcontent.com/pod-product-compliance
Lightning Source LLC
LaVergne TN
LVHW050525100826
845148LV00002B/445

9781425519735